MW01173794

Exodus From The Quicksand

Poetry

By

Reggie Wilson Jr.

First Paperback Edition March 2024

Book design by Reggie Wilson Jr

Cover design by Reggie Wilson Jr.

Edited by Reggie Wilson Jr.

ISBN: 979-8-218-34843-4- Paperback

ISBN: 979-8-218-38830-0- Hardcover

Calreg84@gmail.com

Encourage_rw1912 (Instagram)

Published by Reggie Wilson Jr.

"My pen and journal are the top and bottom lips of my spirit"
Reggie Wilson Jr.

Dedications

For all those in need of encouragement
and
help with self-encouragement, I extend the
pages of my heart to you. Every word plays
the beat of my heart, fighting to stay alive.
I fight to end mental health stigmas and to
express the power of poetry. We all have
something to say, so let us say it. Stay
Encouraged

This book is dedicated to my niece Trinity,
who is the strongest person I know. I see
you baby and I hear you. You teach me
something new about perseverance and
strength every day. I Love you, my love.

Posthumously, Terry Jo (my other mama)
and Tarica (my sister),
Although you both now reside in Heaven,
I pray that all will know that this book was

written with you in mind as well. Miss you both terribly.

To my brother Tony, I pray that we have eternity in Heaven to catch up. This book was written with you in my heart.

To my Great Grandmother Minnie, I do not know how to express your influence. You have been gone for 24 years and yet I still hear your voice ringing in my head. And I thank God for those echoes. I still feel your embrace when I am most in need of it. Salute to you Grandma.

Note to the reader: This book of poetry contains and explores forms of trauma, suicidal ideations, mental health diagnoses/symptoms and encouragement. Be advised.

Foreword

I have seen death. I have also at times wished for it to make another appearance. Not for others but for me. Dealing with things that only I have carried within. Being the caretaker and the bridge but even the bridge needs renovation and caretakers need care. This has always been an issue for me. Born to serve.

Born in Raleigh, North Carolina with purpose in my veins yet my direction evaded me. I searched on my own and found the pen and paper. I can lose myself within ink stains and pencil shavings. I found what I had been looking for. The tools that would be used to stop my own destruction and self-sabotage. This tool from God was used throughout my life but materialized as part of my medicinal regime in 2015. I suffered a horrible asthma attack that resulted in respiratory arrest and life-support twice. This trauma rendered me changed and I found myself questioning why I was alive. Why was I brought back? Why God saved me from the grips of death?

Was I worth it? Dealing with my body not being the same and being quarantined long before the pandemic, I questioned if life would ever be the same. My prime cut down and I woke up a far older man than my age would indicate. Depression, anxiety, posttraumatic stress disorder and constant
suicidal ideations I carried with a smile so no one would notice. And then like a ram in the bush, the gift of the pen called me like Sunday dinner from down the hall. As I found my poetic voice
again, it was revealed that I knew how to knit words and write myself up the hills I was told to look unto to find my
help. Words, analogies, metaphors, and

storytelling, all came pouring out. I was sinking in quicksand, but God gave me a branch to pull myself out of my own warzone of emotions.

Poetry was that tool. I am still writing myself loose from the quicksand, but I can see daylight. I dream that this book of ups, downs, heartbreaks, and hope ENCOURAGES you like it ENCOURAGED me to write it. Allow yourself to get lost in the words and verses, if only for a little while. Thank you for hearing me.

Table of Contents

Purpose

Me Served Warm

My tears are mine,
My memories are mine,
My mistakes are mine,
My pain is mine,
My heartaches are mine,
My past is mine,
My words are yours,
Read them slow.

Hug the words and allow them to hug you back. Hear the words that you want to say. Feel the encouragement that flows through each verse. Let us see and hear each other through these pages. Let us begin our Exodus.

Chapter 1

I am Here

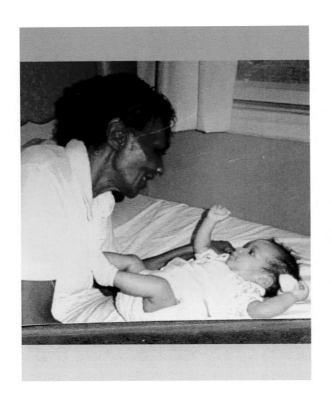

2

Pre-School Negotiation

It felt heavy in my hands,
This Gun,
But almost anything is heavy for a 4-
year-old,
The cold steel excited me like being
tickled or popsicles,
Our friendship was made under
grandma's bed,
It whispered to me and then called
my name,
So, I rescued it from the shoeboxes
and dust and lint that held it captive,

3

My shoulder screamed as I pulled
through the tug war like struggle,
But I won,
With my turtle pajamas being kissed
with dust and hairpins and
mothballs,

I raised my new friend and put it to
my grandma's head,

With a smile on my face,
Playing and replaying moments of
water guns and laser guns that made
funny noises,
I thought this would be the same joy,
and my giggles would be invited by
this beautiful woman,

But horror dripped from her face,

4

A thousand nightmares and
tragedies flashed across her eyes
like
unwanted commercials,
Yet her voice never rose above an
ant's belly,
Her fingertips directing to the
ground put me in a trance like the
smell of
her sweet potato pies would,
Now with two hands, my miniature
phalanges gripped tighter around the
trigger,
"Bang Grandma Bang"
My laughter transported imaginary
shots because her

5

guardian angel held the bullet,

like gauze over rushing blood,
And my angel kept the trigger from
completing its task,
She smiled through her tears,
"Put it down baby, we will play later
okay, come give it to me"
I waddled over to the person that
would become my best friend 11
years later,
The cruel bullet of dementia and old

unapologetic and non-accepted age
got her in the end,

But that day, she was magnificent,

As she lovingly took the gun from my
grasp, she looked up to the ceiling,
Or so I thought,
But she erupted in a praise I still
have never heard,
A praise that suggested that she
thought her life was over at the
hands of her baby,
The oldest of the 4th generation God
instructed her to raise,
Oh, the tears that ran down her face,
like the rivers running from the
Garden of Eden,
The groan that bellowed from the pit
of her stomach reaching her knees,

"Thank you, Lord, have mercy Jesus"

I walked out the room looking for
something else to get into,
But now, I know what I could have
done,
I could have killed the mother of my
family,
The reason I am not to be feared in a
parking deck if I'm seen alone in the
dark,

The reason why I am a southern
gentleman,
The reason why I give is because I
saw her give,
The reason why I am not ashamed of
my Lord and Savior Jesus Christ,
Because I saw Him save her from me,

Thank God for angels,
Arresting and detaining the 4-year-
old long enough for the preschool
negotiator to do her thing,
Once a week, I dream about what
happened that day,
Sometimes the trigger is pulled,
sometimes I cannot find the gun
under the bed,
But all the time, I am screaming "I'm
sorry"And she always says,

"I'm fine son, now go wash your face,
and find your words to write."

Trauma and Truth

Pages of Trauma,
Still Cuts like Papercuts do,
Band-Aids of Hope Reigns

10

Acknowledging the Supplier

God is the ink in my pen that never
runs dry,
He is the majesty of my words that
tells thoughts and wind to confide,
Rocking waves against boats of
fishermen,
While rocking the pages as I fish for
synonyms,
He is the grace between epiphanies,
And hope amongst wordplay and
analogies,
Breakthroughs and deep breathing,
Arms raising and voices singing,
He is in the crevices of my notebook,

Within the canyons and caves of
metaphors that got me shook,

Miracles and unmerited favor

caresses me like a shepherd's
hook.

Prisoner of the Pen

Am I a prisoner or a soldier,
Maybe a delicate mixture,
For I am chained to Poetry,
When she calls, I come,
When she whips me, I scream
affection and delight,
She feeds me life, life that I thought
was lost to me,
When I stray off The Journal
Plantation,
She sends the dogs of rhyme
and free verse after me,
They chase me down every time and
lick my word barren wounds,
While I'm dragged back to the big
house of syllables and metaphors,

13

I hear her singing,
Singing songs in a language only I
can understand,

A special tantalizing, titillating,
tenderizing type of calligraphy,
Poetry kisses me, making my skin
rise like mountainous volcanoes
waiting to burst out with slow gentle
lava of words and majesty,
When my eyes are full of tears and
sight is seldom,

Poetry allows me to hear her through
my fingertips,

14

I survey her volumes like braille, and
I then understand why I have to be in
chains,
Why I must be governed,
Why I need her watchful eye,
My feet, my mouth, my hands
sometimes forget themselves,
I become uncontrollable and
insatiable,
The likelihood of me running just to
proclaim what she taught me to the
world is too high,
Poetry shhhs me,
So am I a prisoner or soldier,
When it is fighting time, I grab my
pen,
I wield it like Excalibur, and I gets to
slicing,

My pen goes on a tangent of
gluttonous wrath,
Eating loose leaf paper like beavers
chewing logs,
Warring against lies and distortions,
Don't fool with my Poetry,
Standing on the front lines for my
Poetry,

Taking bullets and throwing some
back, for my Poetry,
Protecting her like bullet proof saran
wrap,
Posted up in front of her but staying
invisible,
Because that's my place,
See, it is the addiction to her that has
the people falling in love,

16

It is her that changes and saves lives,
Both with brevity and long
windedness like the breeze through
the willow trees in Savannah,
So, I reckon I am a prisoner and
soldier,
For I stay linked to her and I die
every day waiting for her
to whisper reasons to continue to
me,

Her sultry powerful voice plays a
solo   on my eardrums, rhythmically
helping me reach mountaintops of
stanzas,

Rivers of love dripping with ink,

I stay chained only because

I want to be,
I am with her,
Militant, by any means necessary.

Early Table Foes

I said...
When I was young, they said rhymes
without a track was whack,
Without a beat on the lunchroom
table my coolness would be disabled,
But my words flip like Dominique
Dawes,
Bending and twisting in air, no flaws,
Cannot be flawed with God's beats in
my heart,
Soundtrack to my verses, processing
sonnets over pop tarts,

Resume of writing as old as power
points and power rangers,
Kicking and punching air, Balboa
swinging writers block and bully
dangers,

I fix my eyes on the prize with Louie's
trumpet in the background,
Waiting for Gabriel's trumpet,
praying I hear it before my
empty pen is found,
So, they were wrong, pens run the
world with words,
Who else writes emotions
and feelings cutting the history with
ink dripping swords,
Sharp as the lightning strikes across
my eyes,

20

Now a man, where my words are
stashed in heavy supply,

Like a battle rapper, I am nosed to
nose,
Entourage of angels around me,

Every bar hits my foes.

Cereal Mission

I wake up with words and metaphors
on my mind,
Pain, pleasure and passion all
defined,
Like filling cereal bowls,
Each spoonful is mine.

Behind Eyelids

I see shelves of poetry books
outlining like wallpaper behind my
eyelids,
So many that they illuminate the
darkest corners of my closed eyes,
Sprinkled with lantern light and
torches burning slow,
The future I want, the dream I have,
They sing to me from the shadows
like crickets in the country,
Sounding board of my childhood,
Volumes and volumes of precious
consolidated vowels and consonants
already to be read,

Every blink, daydream, nap and goodnight sleep invite my true love,

Creating a house of words carefully crafted for encouragement.

Chapter 2

It Started with Belief

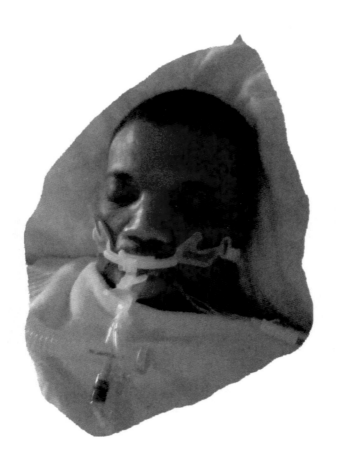

26

Identification

I am a Black man,
Fell out my mama's womb, a Black
Man,
Wrapped in a blanket, a Black Man,
And grew as a Black Man,
But to you, I'm just the identifiable
Black Male,
To you I'm just him and not me,
Call me what I am, what I've always
been,
A Black Man,
Identified by the grace of my God and
the blood of my mama,
A Black Man.

27

Reawakening

Revival is Here
Rebirth and the Renaissance
Resurrection Now.

The Porcupine's Journey

I am encapsulated by the splinters of
the Cross,
The Cross that I pick up and carry
every day,
Splinters sticking out from me, I am
barely recognizable anymore,
I am a porcupine, waiting the
seconds and inches and minutes and
miles of this tedious journey,
I have been walking for a long time,
With blood circling my tear ducts,
Squeezing each rough sandpaper-like
memory over my bruised and
battered cheekbones,
I am mesmerized by the pain,

Pain so great that it lulls me to sleep
with its dullness,

It wakes me up with its sharpness,

But trouble for me is impossible to
last always,
Yet still the beast of life often
swallows me in its belly,
Saturated with the acid rain dripping
from the walls of its belly,
My skin burns where the splinters of
the Cross have found kissable
partners with my epidermis,
Yet I always wait,
Wait on the Lord like Psalm 27
expressed,

As I full-court press Heaven with
prayers as mighty as the shouts of
faith that caused Jericho to fall,
I go through slippery wet streets, but
I stand steadfast in the order of my
ordered steps,

My steps are blessed, yet remnants
of damp tissues and discounted hope
fills the prints my size twelves leave
behind, I march through the
wilderness anyway,
With the splinters from the Cross on
my back,
I am a billboard for my God's LLC,
Battle torn but still forever a warrior
poet I was born.

31

Harp Lesson

The strings of the harp sings to me,
With notes that bend the test of time
and outline the arc of life,
Those long gone no longer play with
fingertips of challenge and courage,
For the notes they played comes from
memories of soundtracks from long
ago,
Each chin and smile waves sweetly in
my direction,
I'm saturated with tears both of
sadness and joy,
Yet the music plays on,
Through the echoes of the past that
forgives the present,
I hear the song,

32

My smile holds the peace that
surrounds this orchestra,

With arms aching to hold,
Oh, how I wonder, how I wonder,
Can I hold on to these notes a little
while longer,
May they hold onto me? I will play by
ear the song sung to me,
I will not waver nor faint.

Waiting for the Sun to Smile

I read "Let not your heart be
troubled"
These words have resided inside a
heart often troubled,
Troubled with thoughts and
memories of trouble,
Reading the words on my heart
spelling out with bold letters
"T-R-O-U-B-L-E"
I want patience, patience and
patience,
Am I having trouble reading my
heart correctly?
But what does all that mean to a
heart that is troubled,

Is there even enough time to
encourage this heart?

Heart filled with troubling tears and
troubled passions,

But I was told to not let my heart be troubled,

I need patience, patience and patience,
Intentionality is needed for these troublesome thorns,
I got patience, patience and patience,

Because I read somewhere "Let not your heart be troubled."

I am Not a Mistake

I am here, all of me, I am here,
Pushed through the womb of life and
love into a world of decay,
Yet I am here,
Full of dreams and hope, like a nest
full of eggs,
Like the sky full of blue and hearts
full of beats,
I am here,
Like streams of prayers rolling from
centuries of triumphs and failures
yet,

I am here,
All of me,
I am here,

Made for this,
Made for me,
Made for someone,

Made to achieve,
Made to imagine like clouds and run
like shooting stars in the sky,
I am not a mistake,
I am here,
All of me.

Enduring

You think you can stop me?
This pain I feel now is only
temporary like so many of life's
horrors,
But you cannot break me,
This sorrow I feel now will not be
constant,
I may hurt sometimes, I might be
hurting now but,
I will heal,
What?
Did you think you held power over
me?
Did you think that you could control
my joy?

Did you actually believe that my
heart would stop beating because you
tried to crush it?
The confusion I am in now will clear
like fog after the
dawn has been chased away by the
day's plan,

Do not think that this confused state
coupled with its partner depression
will sink me in a watery grave full of
my tears,
Never,
You must know that I will not
succumb to your beatings,
I will not die due to your slander,

Mortality will not be feared or
lamented because of the pain,
sorrow, confusion or depression,

I am too strong plus my soul will fly
with the angels and kneel at His
throne,
So
I am enduring,
And you think you can stop me?

41

Stay Encouraged

42

I'm able to see Me

I'm able to dance on the rays of the
sun,
And walk smoothly in the moonlight,
I'm able to battle hatred with swords
of love,
And climb mountains with shoes of
persistence,
I'm able to float on the breath of God,
And breathe in words of wisdom,
I'm able to swim through my tears,
And wade in the water of my
mother's dreams,
I'm able to be who I was created to
be,

And who I am, my mama said, was enough.

You told Me

You told me that I was special,
That there was no one greater in the
whole wide world,
You said that I was going to be a good
man,
A man you felt blessed to help raise,
You told me not to boast but to know
that I am a king,
A king that should reign with
strength and love,
Flowing upwards to the Heavens
with the love of God in my heart,
You told me that the torch was mine,
To light the world with my light,

This lil light of mine was what you lulled me to sleep with,

Always to let my let shine you said,
Always to know that I am a gem, a gem worth displaying,
That I glowed like the red moon on a clear night,
You told me that I was a star, sparkling bright and blazing,

A flower growing beautiful and stretching to the sun,

To soar like an eagle and be wise as an owl,
To run fast as a cheetah from evil,

46

And to be slow enough to appreciate
God's blessings,
To fully understand when someone's
love is helpful,
And to fully discern when someone's
love is hurtful and harmful,
To be a captain of my own ship and
steer to the shore of success,
You told me to be faithful like Joshua
marching through the wilderness,
To be forever a resident of the
Promised Land.

Unbroken

I fix my eyes on them hills I read
about at the edge of grandma's bed,
Hearing her recite triumphs and
tribulations from wonders and
nightmares of her past,
Yet in still she said "look to the hills
baby, that's where my help comes
from"
Floating on clouds of wonder and
surfing through currents as swift as
my imagination,
Climbing, mountaintops thought to
be unreachable and grabbing the
wind still invisible,
Yet the promises from hills have
fortified me grandma,

Just like you said they would,
With boots laced tight with miracles
holding them together,

I march with purpose and passion,
never wavering for the promises
never failed me,
Hearts break, cars break, bones
break, but never my God's word,
That little boy was paying attention
grandma, now a man of God,

Fighting the good fight you won
already,
Unbroken.

Sermon in the Bed

I sleep amongst the scriptures,
My pillowcases are laced with verses
not my own,
But they are still mine,
Intertwined like fine linen sheets
that I repeat dreams in,
Night after night I stay covered up,
From Genesis through Revelation
keeping my head to my toes warm,
The whining of springs in my
mattress keeps me aware of tempting
temptations that often call when the
moon is bright,
They sing the songs of Potiphar's wife
and Delilah,

Softly hitting high notes in my ears
and tattooing evil plans across my
chest,

Lord, where are the Proverbs?
Where are Psalms, where is my
Ruth?
You see I sleep amongst the
scriptures,
The only way I can walk by faith in
the morning,
One step in Noah's ark and the other
in Jonah's great fish,
Either way I am going to need this
Bible study bed,
Resting blindly on my personal
Damascus Road.

Positive Affirmation Confirmation

A man full of empathy and kindness,
Flowing through streams of
compassion and dripping with hope,
Walking through endless days of
opposition and enemy attacks,
While never giving in or up,
Never losing my light,
Resiliency has been my shield and
my helmet,
The protection of positive
stubbornness,
Never allowing bullets, axes, swords
or arrows of negativity to puncture
my well-meaning heart,

I am too much, too much of all the
good things,

My feet are rehearsed to enter the
war for love's sake,
My heart beats the beats of the dream
my mother dreamt,
The sparkle of her eye gave me the
fireworks in mine,
I fly with the power of an eagle while
my spirit surveys all,
Who is this man,

Man of valor,
Man of passion,
Man of reasoning,
Man of love,
He is I,

Encouragement and empathy
personified,
He is I.

Like Joseph

Like Joseph I have been...
Mistreated and Honored,
Forgotten and Favored,
Disrespected and Respected,
Sneered and Cheered,
Stepped on and Raised up,
Vilified and Praised,
Hurt and Hugged,
Frowned at and Smiled at,
Forsaken and Cherished,
Deprived and Nourished,

Tortured and Comforted,
Discouraged and Encouraged,
Like Joseph I have been Hated and
Loved

55

And Like Joseph,
I am Set Apart.

UP on High

The taker is UP,
The giver is UP,
So, I have to look UP,
My praise goes UP,
I send my prayers UP,
Hands raised sky UP,
Time for shame been UP,
Test for self-hating, pencils down,
times UP,
Hallelujahs shake things UP,
Like eagles I mount UP,
Spirit waiting charged UP,
Listening for the trumpet, excited to
float UP,
Opposite of down like lightning
striking UP.

Stay Encouraged

58

Picking up Feathers

The hidden treasure of goals and
dreams cascade and descend all
around me,
Through frustrations and
condemnation, I still can't help but to
reach,
Reach for what calls me,
Millions of feathers on the ground
and I don't have to be flightless,
As I find a pair of feathers that fits, I
take off,
I soar to my goals and dreams and
grab at them with talons of purpose
and discernment,
Out flying the bullets from below and
pressing on,

Emancipated from the hunters hopes
of ending my hopes,
Yet I still reach for what calls me,

With every chest compression my
wings flap and clap over creation,
Ever present and evergreen with my
goals and dreams in my talons.

Who Won?

I am the one,
Under the sun,
Who won before time begun,

Made in the Image of the Son,
The race is now done,
I have won, I have won,

I am the one
On top of the lighted sun,

So, who won?

I won.

Love Letter to Me

Stronger than Samson himself, I am,
Piercing eyes bouncing off the sun
like waves off the coast of the
Atlantic,
Walking and trembling the tectonic
plates below,
Stretching the land mass into several
pieces with each toe purposely
planted,
Battle tested and scarred from head
to toe,
But my mama said scars tell a story,
A story of struggle and wonder,
Like a jigsaw puzzle or game of
connect the dots,
My scars scream my story,

12 inches across my stomach, a dent
in my head and cuts and staples
constructing the melanin
Frankenstein of the king that I am,

Royalty running marrow deep,
Coming out of Eden by way of the
South,
Breathing honesty, compassion, and
love,
Love not needing decoding, but just
is,

A man of empathy singing deep down
through the Red Sea like Paul
Robeson,
But can reach high up Mt. Everest
like Eddie Kendricks,

All with two feet made for the
wilderness,
Swimming against the current of my
nightmares,

With sword and shield in both hands,
Reciting Psalms and parables,
Tongue of fire and water,
Me be Me.

I am a Man of God

I am a man forged from the same dirt
Adam was made from,
Draped in favor as Joseph was,
Protected and rescued like Peter and
Paul,
As strong as Samson and wise as
Solomon,
Longsuffering as Job,
Beloved as David and as dedicated as
Joshua,
Abraham like blessed wrapped in
Jacob's birthright,
I am a Man,
He and Him.

Chapter 3

Thank You

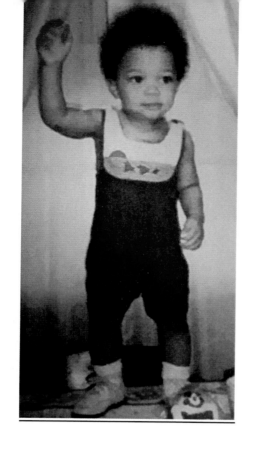

Veins

Waving with Full Veins
Generations of Breakthroughs
Together We Here.

Minnie Flight of Peace

I heard a lullaby in my dreams last
night,
So loud and beautiful that it rocked
me out of bed,
I hit the floor softly landing on the
same cotton that she picked,
I floated to the ceiling encased with
smells of vindication,
Pressing through the ceiling like
airplanes infusing with clouds,
My eyes glazed with thoughts and
memories I thought were lost to me,
The lullaby sings me upward,
upward, upward,

Your voice pierces my side,
reminding me of Your sacrifice,

Passing the atmosphere now where
sound cannot be heard,
And yet, I hear You,
Holding the hand of hers,
Welcoming me home,
I wonder Jesus, if I became the man
she thought I would be by now,
The man she prayed to You I would
be,

As I drift with heavenly aim and
purpose across burning balls of gas
and the radiant sun,

I'm still at peace,
That Isaiah 26: 3 peace,

That no understanding peace,
That real peace,
As my spirit and soul drips still
waters from River Jordan,
I see her, thank You Jesus, I see her,
The one that left breadcrumbs for me
to find You Jesus,
The singer of the lullaby You wrote
the lyrics for,
Am I what you prayed I would be
grandma?

I bear the markings of the Lord
Jesus, so I know I am supposed to be
here,
But how did I do on earth grandma?
Where the sun don't always give
warmth and where the kindness of

my eyes didn't always shine
excellently,
Where my hope and self-love has not
come easy for me,

I miss you grandma, so much,
I miss your lap where my head felt
comfort,

I miss your voice,
I thought I was forgetting you,
It has been so long,
I'm sorry I blamed you for dying and
leaving me,
For leaving a family that needed you,
I'm so sorry,
Smiles and tears of joy, joyously
striking down her recreated heavenly
cheeks like Gabriel's trumpet,

Waiting to burst with praise for my
ultimate graduation,

Now I am home, eternally at peace,
counting my crowns at the Master's
feet,

Side by side,
With grandma,
I must have done good, right
grandma?
I mean I did just hear Well Done.

Pure Courage 101

As strong as the cough medicine you
made me take when I was little,
coughing and wheezing,
As strong as your arms holding me
before every sleepless night as the
beeping of machines sustaining my
life grew louder and often
infrequent,
As strong as the prayers shouting the
pleas of every solitary tear, racing,
and tripping over each other down
each cheek,
As strong as the plug staring at you
ominously encouraging you to pull it,
As strong as the doctor's fore arms,
biceps and triceps were

beating and pushing on my chest and tubes down my throat,

Thoughts of potential gone, lost and wasted,
But then, 1 beat, 2 beat, 3 beat, beats of a heart long forgotten about, lungs long ago reporting empty, sorry no air here,
Suddenly they too were open for business,

Your strength, your love, your tears made me courageous for what better teacher of courage, than the one who had me in a hospital, only to lose me and welcome me again in the same hospital,
Curious Courage,

I'm courageous because I'm your son
and you my brave mama.

A Mother's Gaze

Eye opening fresh from birth,
Gazing into the eyes of wisdom and a
life spent gathering,
Gathering tools, skills and memories
of wins and a few defeats,
Piercing light flashes while cold air
never felt before rushes over newly
developed skin,
Being born feels different,
The womb encapsulated a unique
support system all too familiar, but...
But now these new eyes examining
down at mine play another role,
The role of honesty, integrity, and
discernment,

Eyes that will lead and encourage
and provide consequences and
rewards,

The birth of a new dawn,
The life of a new day,
The heart made to be loved by these
eyes of wisdom and a life spent
gathering.

My Other Great Love

Laughter a mile long, trust as deep as
deep can be,
Fashioned together with that angelic
voice and smile,
I can remember your laugh so warm
like cake from the oven,
Now the memory of it pierces me like
a heavenly bee sting,
Sweet but hurts,
How can memories be hopeful and
hurtful at the same time?
And yet, it makes sense,
The pain makes memories
memorable and the beauty of
remembering you makes the bee
sting worth it,

I hate that you are gone without me
being able to kiss your forehead,

Protocol and quarantines kept me
away like a forcefield,
But I need to believe that my love was
strong enough to crash through the
barricades and hold your hand,
I hope you felt it and knew that you
were safe, and your son was there.

My Reasons: Nieces and Nephews

I am your hero?
Really?
Me?
Always grabbing my hand,
Sitting in my lap,
Whispering in my ear,
Asking questions,
Telling me secrets,
Big secrets, small secrets, any type of
secrets,
Hugs that never loosen,
Hugs that constrict with love,
acceptance and understanding,
And you say I am your hero?
Really?
Me?

81

Your encouragement, your empathy,
your attention and your confidence
in me shines through,

You highlight my life and purpose,
My arms ache with loneliness when
they are not holding you,
My eyes water with tears of Heaven
when I see you,
My reasons to continue,
You are mine and more fantastically,
I am yours,

Like sharks, movies and sleep,
Swimming, entertaining and
rejuvenating my lungs,
My heroes, Yes you,
Always and always you.

My Backbone is You

Being sold for gold, was getting old,
out in the cold, even for the bold, so I
am told,
Anger from being raped was caped,
and carefully shaped by the
revelation of the escape,
A face masked with blood, made to
crawl in the mud, only to wash their
children with suds,
They broke your nose when
resistance you chose, but from your
head to your toes, still stronger than
your foes,
They called you dirty wench and that
your seeds would never get off the
bench,

Not human enough to eat, drink or sit with them, but human enough to please them and nurse them,

Elevator drivers, maids, and cooks, midwives and Sunday school teachers, nurses and keepers of books,
Jobs you took seriously despite their condescending looks,
Watching folks with black milk running through their veins, hurting and killing, leaving on the pavement sad stains, as you sweetly prayed for their pains,

Now they want your precious children, those that grew within, they

84

want them out of your house, where
they always been,
But you fight, never flight, until
everything was all right and every
one of your children was in sight,
Being sold for gold, was getting old,
out in the cold, even for the bold, so I
am told,
But in you my dear grandmother, I
am consoled.

MMMMMMMM

MMM MMMM MMM MMMMMM
Grandma said to hum when you do
not have the words cause Jesus
knows what you say through the
groans,
MMM MMMM MMM MMMMMM
I testify my heart and my lungs
through my fingertips,
My fingertips encapsulating the
evidence of my fearfully and
wonderfully made conception,
The faucets of my praise,
Pouring from the heart's river,
Over smooth stones formed and
organized by the Holy Spirit,

With architectural perfection
pointing to the fingers holding my
pen,

Destination paper where being
ashamed is abolished,
Grandma said to never be ashamed
to praise Him,
To lift my head and call to the hills
from which cometh my help,
Well, I'm not ashamed,
Not ashamed to admit that I live on
the hill,

Desperately wanting to get closer,
Pressing my way up Calvary,

Smelling like smoke from the fiery
furnaces of life,
And the smell of sheep in the fields,
Fur from a lion's mane still in my
hair from all these dens,
Yet my God saw me through,
MMM MMMM MMM MMMMMMM,
The rocks stay mad at me, for I am
selfish,
I need to praise him, so they are
commanded to stay quiet,
No crumb of mountains will steal
what is mine,
I testify with my pen, waist deep in
His Word,

I cry out through the wilderness,

Tears in my heart, joy and fire on my
tongue,
MMM MMMM MMM MMMMMMM.
Like your

Chocolate Love Cake
Baked with Love and Heaven's Peace
Grandma's Classic Joy,
Any Holiday, Every Holiday
I Waited for its Glory
Any Holiday, Every Holiday, Yes, I
did,
The Smell of Passion

The Sweet Smell of Perfection
The Smell of Patience,
The Taste of Greatness
Rich with Character and Love
Plates always Overflowing,
Forks and Spoons, Spoons and Forks
Tastebuds working Overtime
Me with Smiles and Grins,
Delicious and Good
Wonderful and Fantastic
Hopeful Prayers Answered,

Missing your Sweet Love
Missing your Kindness and Grace
The Mercy of Cake
Chocolate Heaven.

90

Sister Mountain

This beauty marries the hardship of
lifegiving,
Persevering through thorn laden
vines wrapping around the ankles of
Genesis,
With courage of power and
vindication pouring from warriors
like Harriet Tubman,
Marching through life and streams
of anger,
Disappointment and disrespect,

With a crowned head, this queen
with royal hands strong like ever
present arms of comfort,
Songs of resilience spring forth like
Jackie Joyner Kersee,

And unyielding like Whitney
Houston's falsetto,
Lifesavers and life givers in one
vessel dripping with eternal pens of
birth encrusted dreams,

Thank you, Sister Mountain

God's Flower

God's flower, laced head to toe with
grace and purpose,
Now forever wrapped in joy with
eternal happiness,
I can hear your laughter through the
floorboards of Heaven,
I can feel your peace through the love
you left us, like precious and ordered
footprints,
Tarica Lynn, your name will never
leave our hearts,
Forever growing in our garden of
heartfelt memories.

I Look Good in Pink

Baby, try not to worry, you don't have
to cry
Son, I look good in pink,
Doctor told me my road is long,
But son, I look good in pink,
Radiation and frustration, chemo
and tears flow,
Look here, I look good in pink,
I'm still strong but I'm tired,
I'm thankful for my left eyelid always
being the first to open,
I'm thankful for my right eyelid
never too proud to follow,
I'm thankful for power in my hands,

94

I'm thankful for peace in my feet,
The journey, the journey, the
journey,

My wilderness is laced with pain and
yet I dance through it all,
So, baby try not to worry, you don't
have to cry,
The fact is, I look good in pink.

Ode to Aunt Renee

I Heard You

"Close that screen door boy"
Was the soundtrack of my childhood,
"Don't let the air out, don't let the
flies in"
"I ain't heating up the neighborhood"
"Close that screen door boy"
Every day in every season,
Same old thing,
Same old chorus,
I smile now but it was annoying then
like the snitching streetlight used to
be,

But I miss those voices,
Prayerfully the screen door
protecting my memories will never
slam in my face.

Under the Streetlight

Bicycles flying through the nights
air,
Mosquito whispers and car horns
providing the soundtrack of my
youth,
Counting to ten with eyes closed,
Seeking and hiding, hiding and
seeking,
Love letters passing, check yes or no,
Basketball bouncing and people
screaming "THAT'S A FOUL",
Jump ropes and water guns, double
dutching and double clutching,
Racing to the mailbox down the
street with head start,

mixed with laughter and untied
shoes,

Fist flying and hugs giving,
Tragedies and triumphs all shared
under the streetlight, dimming the
light of a thousand lightning-bugs,
Days and nights have brought
pleasure and pain,

Rest and resiliency,
Patience and perseverance,
All learned under the streetlight.

Stay Encouraged

100

Butterscotch Pew

Yellow orange golden spheres of
taste kissing joy,
Making church as a boy easy,
Learning how to be quiet,
Unwrapping secretly as I could,
"Crinkle Crackle"
Mama's eyes fixed and glaring,
Pupils awaiting to tattletale to her
ears,
The eyes were always two reliable
witnesses waiting to testify on me in
between testimonies,
But my enemy has always been
mama's ears,
They always were a pair of snitches,

A pinch reminded me of the
hardships of not sitting beside the
cool auntie,

My ears encapsulated by a chorus of,
"Shhhhhhhhhs".

You Tried It

You said she praised God too loud,
You couldn't hear the sermon,
You said she stood up too much,
You couldn't see the pastor you said,
Her clapping and Hallelujahing was
louder than the choir,
You couldn't hear your favorite song,
You said, "it don't take all that",
But,
You couldn't see her story for fear
you would be praising with her,
You don't know that she once rode a
horse and like Paul was knocked off
of it,

You don't know the pain and loss she
suffered,

103

Like DNA under fingertip and throats
scarred from screaming,
You don't know the angels she
recognized fighting the demons she
didn't,
You don't know how blessed she felt
to have a Savior after living a life
with few heroes,
No, you don't know,

And if you did, you would get up and
praise right beside her,
And if you don't like it,
Move to another pew, get closer to
pulpit,
Sing in the choir, or simply,
Focus on Jesus,
And less on my family,

We are going no where cause God
never left us,
No church hurt will stop her praise,
For she lives what she preached,
And that was to never be ashamed to
praise the Lord,
Besides, you never say anything to
her face anyway,
So, change pews already and leave
mine alone.

Flat Tops and Fades

Sitting in the barber's chair I learned
many things,
Free lollipops and older men eating
fish sandwiches,
All with smiles full of teeth,
Some not so full,
Someone fussing on the phone, tele
not cell,
Others angry because of the heat,
But really its anger due to waiting in
line,
The line, the line, the line,
Sounds of clippers and pages flipping
searching for the beauty of the week,

All getting ready for graduation, weddings, school pictures and job interviews
Me the flat top and you the fade.

Summer Forever

My mind wonders through an
endless maze of sea breezing
possibilities,
Wading in tall grasses of certainty
and compromise,
Hiding beneath a tall and comforting
willow tree, Shading my eyes from
the piercing of the sun,
I enjoy shade,
Now feeling the cool earth under my
feet, my two heels, my ten toes
dancing and vibrating,
My eyes gazing to the sky as blue as
my feelings were before this
vacation,

Sifting through shifting intangible
tangible clouds of glory and wonder,
Tears of sorrow and strength,
tragedy, and triumph, of dreams and
nightmares, of horrors and hopes,

of hates and loves,

These tears fall from my eyes like
boulders from a cliff and crashing.
down my cheeks like a stream of
living resumes,

Resting under this willow tree
overlooking the sea,
The sea that I see,
Sneezing through every present
allergy from the grass that cradles
me with yellow snow throughout,

109

It both loves and hates me, I both
love and hate it,
Yet I do not want to leave it,
This grass, this soil, these trees, this
sea, this sky and all these clouds
above me, as I float in endless pools,

No, I do not want to leave, I do not
want to leave,
Do not make me leave, I love this
summer, summer of life, summer of
forever, summer of Savannah
Georgia, the summer that made
sense,
Vacation so ideal because it was my
REAL.

After School Appointments

Smells like play dough and red Kool-
Aid,
The stickiness of Band-Aids,
Skint knees and potato chip breath,
Fresh cut grass and the dance
between salty tears and sweat,
Sweet hugs and love notes from the
neighborhood,
Bullies and best friends sharing
blocks,
Shout dichotomously but natural,
Like fist and friends,
Pollen making yellow snow covering
cars that marks base,

**Saving those from being it,
Hiding and seeking, Kickball and
racing to the mailbox,**

**Dodging the snakes of life and the
mosquitoes of nightmares,**

It is home.

Chapter 4

Heartbreak Led to Hope

114

Stain of My Heart

Tattoo of love stains my heart,
I say stain because it is a mess,
A mess I want cleaned, extracted,
and blotted away,
It follows me constantly,
Making even the thought of it
unbearable,
It is beginning to stink,
The stench has enveloped my heart,
I want this tattoo gone,
I want it gone forever,
Why would I ever consider this,
My heart was clean,was stain proof
but now it needs a power wash,What
was I thinking? Tattoos can last.

Thorny Rose

What hurts and stings like a thorny
rose,
So beautiful yet dangerous like a
beautiful jaguar,
So sweet yet bitter like sour candy,
It must be handled with care,
Must be allowed to breathe,
Can't crowd it,
The thorny rose can only be realized
from a distance,
Only the entranced eyes are allowed
to roughly handle it,
Red beauty runs down the thorny
rose like water into the hands and
fingers and veins of the unwise,

The heart of man bleeds the sweet
fragrance of the thorny rose,

The smell last longer than the blood
can flow,

The red beauty of the thorny rose
is a killer,
Love is its weapon of choice,
Bitter at the taste of the ills of the
world that was force fed to her,
But sweet at the prospect of
greatness.

Serving Waffles

Only allowing to see what I want you
to see,
Shapeshifting and remodeling my
structure and color scheme like an
octopus and chameleon,
With each step I am losing me
though,
The passion for the passionless
renders me excommunicated from
the world I want for myself,
My voice is different, an
impersonation from the ultimate
people pleaser,
I am the dummy that sits and waits to
be talked through,

118

Feeling invalidated by the
ventriloquist,
I have forgotten my voice like so
many forgotten notes and words of
songs,

I lip-sing,
But when I am alone,
I am sexy and my voice is beautiful
like the perfect amount of maple
syrup inside each square of a warm
waffle,
It is time I shared this breakfast,

The breakfast of me,
Whomever wants a plate, take it,
Whomever does not,
Leave it on the table,
Or me on the table.

The Olive Tree

Come meet me at the olive tree,
If you want to find me that's where
I'll be,
Sitting under its comfort and
protection,
Waiting for you and praying against
your rejection,
Humming songs that you might want
to hear,
Whistling words from my heart and
feeling no fear,
Tapping my chest with my fingers,
The thought of us under this olive
tree lingers,
Where are you, are you coming?

120

That fact that I'm still waiting is
stunning, It's getting late and still no
you,
Maybe you don't love me,
Maybe that's true.

Salt from Tears

I want a do over,
Perfectionism,
Reliving decisions already made,
Recidivism,
Eyes focused backwards,
Moonwalking,
Sucking up salt from tears,
Vacuuming,
Haters hating and separating,
Jim Crow,
Cowards of past episodes small,
So so,
Watching the waves of the tide roll
in, Foam,
Processing my thoughts in my head,
Dome,

Playing my heart strings,
Songs,
Shouting skywards,
Tongues.

Cumulonimbus

Dreams in the clouds,
There isn't anything more pressing
and worthwhile like my dreams,
As abundant as the heart strings
from a loving mother, and as
precious as the first sight of a
newborn,
My dreams seem far away though,
but I can see them like clouds, ever
moving across blue tinted skies,
Racing, racing, racing,
As I try to catch up to these dreams, I
am reminded by the sweet-smelling
flowers under my feet,
The flowers of my now, my today, my
present,

Flowers populated and smiling back
at me like memories begging not to
fade,

As I bend down to smell and sniff my
now, my today and my present, I look
up and notice that my clouds of
dreams are waiting for me,
The images of a future I crave, my
desires smile back at me,
They sing a chorus exclaiming
encouragement,

Clouds urge me to smell my now and
to not give up on it,
The clouds cheer me on to smell my
today and fight until my today
mirrors my clouds,

125

They also clap for me to unwrap my
   present as if it was a present,

The dreams in the clouds promised
me that they would wait for me, if I
take time to smell my flower of now
                  and today,
One flower at a time, one petal at a
                     time,
I'm encapsulated by my clouds, and
           I'm comforted.

Masterpiece

Sweet breezes on top of elegant
mountain tops,
Sprayed by dazzling and glorious
snowflakes,
Melting into amiable streams of pure
water,
Flowing down curvy rocky trails,
Covering every specific and
individual pebble,
Enveloped by soft sand dug deep
within the ravenous mountain in the
middle of a valley,
Rich with sunflowers and piercing
green blades,
Providing a buffet for the heavenly
beautiful rabbits,

Feasting under an oak tree offering
shade from the radiant sun,

Hiding behind thin clouds with
peaking rays staring through the
spaces,
With wind encapsulated by the sweet
fragrances of the perfect breeze.

New Breeze

The air of new dawn mixed with the
sight of the passing night,
A new breeze is coming,
Through sunsets of lyrics and the
harmonizing of past triumphs,
A new breeze is coming,
Majestic beats of worthy hearts
pound the warrior cry of the
vindicated.
A new breeze is coming,
Over the hill and through the valley
soaked with dew and tears,
Yet,
A new breeze is coming,
Fog lifted, sight renewed, troubled
waters calmed,

129

Peace be still,
A new breeze is coming,

And I will be here to meet it,
Like paper to my words.

Crush

I dreamt of you before I fell asleep
last night,

Dreams of your hair interrupting my
plans for tomorrow,

Intertwining my fingers and
interlocking my imagination,

I dreamt of you,

The highways of your integumentary
system I travel with the radio playing
my heartbeat,

I know all the detours,

Every canyon and misty stream
landmarks hopes and wishes of
forehead touches,

I dreamt of you last night,

My eyes were wide open.

Breathing Dreams

Dreaming is like breathing,
As you inhale, you dream and dream,
As you exhale, you release a dream,
The problem comes when you cannot
breathe at all
The issue comes when you cannot
dream anymore,
Priceless are dreams,
Precious as air,
Dreaming is the air that is needed to
oxygenate our desires,
Lungs represented by our present
and future,
Both dreaming and breathing are
priceless and precious

133

gifts not meant to be thwarted,

Misused, abused, forgotten, ignored,
or doubted,
Most essential,
Most important,
Most needed,
Shake off the mud from yesterday
and find new boots to stomp through
the muck and mire,
Breathe in new air and encapsulate
your dreams with compassion,
Do not waste them,
Let wisdom reign and light your own
peaceful monarchy.

History of Hope

Pressing onwards, from the
streetlights of my childhood,
Through the pothole infested streets,
Under bridges and over overpasses,
All in search of hope,
Hope that lights creation,
Presently and pleasantly,
Like a carousel of affirmation.

Dear Mr. Quicksand

Why are you stuck?
The footprints of comparisons are
deep and devastatingly smothering
like a spider's web,
You are often trapped, never seeing
your worth due to counting the worth
of others,
You are sinking,
The more you fight and struggle inch
by inch your heart sinks deeper and
deeper,
Minimization and perfectionism
have become your bodyguards,
Shielding you from the
acknowledgment of your

136

greatness, like your great grandma
believed,

Yet you are in quicksand, running in
place and going nowhere, like salt
trying to escape the sea or the clouds
fighting against the sky,
Comparisons are holding your
ankles, rejections grasp your knees,
hatred wraps around your waist and
self-doubt strangles your neck,
Why not live like the sunflowers do,
following the sun,
Why not be like the water in a stream
or the stones at the bottom, content
in the majesty of the creator,

Why not fly like the birds of the air
with feathers touched by arrows of
flames,
Forever soaring over the pits of
despair of the sands pulling down
quick.

I See Me

How does one fall in love with
oneself?
Is there a manual of a blueprint for
this endeavor?
Laying a brick road towards my
heart,
Knocking on the door and ringing the
doorbell with flowers and candy,
Or,
Calling myself and pillow talking or
hitting myself up in my own direct
messages,
Liking my own pictures and kissing
the mirror before I go to sleep,
Is this how it should work?
To gaze upon my own handiwork and
smile,

Smile like a baby finding a noisy toy,

I will be heard,
Only to find myself at odds with what
the world tells me,
Like braille, the world leaves bumps
in my spirit for me to read,
Decoding messages all my own,

Where can I go to view myself as I
should,
To marry myself with conviction and
privilege,
I owe myself Myself,
Even if others can't see me and or
willingly blind themselves,
I vow to love and adore myself,
From toes to bald head,
Poet you are loved.

Chapter 5

Encouraged
by Resiliency

142

Blood Cheer Hopeful

I look for stars in the sky of my mind,
Processing the sea of blood that I'm
swimming through,
With every breaststroke I notice the
shore,
The shore covered with dreams and
goals given to me,
I get lost with the current twisting
and turning my mind like a feather in
the wind,
I'm drowning stained with ruby
colored liquid,
With my last remaining seconds of
breath holding, I hear a cheer,

A cheer from inside my heart
screaming, kick on, float, kick, float,
kick,
I kick zealously to the surface
searching for the shore,

The darkness has fallen and sight
impossible,
But I keep kicking and floating in the
blanket of night,
Yet I see it,
The sparkle of a lighthouse named
HOPEFUL,

Guiding me to the shore,
I see it,
The light, I see it,
I am hopeful, with cheer in my heart
and blood stained.

Round Forever

"Last Round" the ref proclaims to
each corner of the ring,
Blood now dripping like a consistent
faucet,
Eyes no longer visible and bottom lip
bigger since round 6,
Booing from the crowd overflowing
the ring like cascading weighted
blankets,
Cups and debris scattered
throughout the ring like children's
toys,
While knees stuck in place on the
stool in the corner,

Towels stained with rose colored platelets,

Nose bent to the left and cuts deep as
the dead sea,

Red flashes of streams sprinkled like
freckles across the ref's shirt,
Memories appearing and
disappearing,
One after the other.

"Last round" and I cannot get off the
stool in the corner,
I hear the ref, but the voice seems so
far away,
I've made my money,
I put on a show,
Fighting for my life with broken
hands hidden by my gloves,
Boo crowd if you must,

Hey Ref, I'm done, I do not want to
be champion anymore,
Give it to the kid to carry,

This torch is getting heavy,
And I'm ready to pass it,
Ribs crushed like dry noodles,
And breath is escaping my lungs like
the last day of school,
Ring the bell and raise his hands,
Someone lift me off the stool,
Carry me back on my shield.

148

Burnout, Anthills and Gravity

The mockingbird yawns,
Faithful he sings, now tired,
Tired of the song,
Wheezing and coughing,
Chest like fire and brimstone,
Air eating red ants infest lungs,
Tears fall all around,
Shovel or rake them all.

Off Key Love

Heartbeats tapping like the Nicholas
Brothers,
Running like Luther's voice,
In perfect motion like the Pips,
Like,
Performers of perfection in my
dreams only highlights the offbeat,
Out of tune,
Lack of rhythm that was your love,
The love you gave me like a skipping
track on my favorite cd,
Staccato like inconsistency,
BOO BOOOO BOOOOOOOO
Screams the essence of my internal
Apollo,

**Eternally get off my stage,
Call the man with the sand.**

Slow Running Maple Syrup

Silently sitting in a chair for turning
and twisting,
Thinking about which shapes the
clouds are posing in outside,
I am stuck inside,
With the dichotomy of dusty
hardwood floors,
Kissing carpets lettered with
notebooks of words,
Staring at chargers meant to give
new life,
Remembering when I was plugged
up, no air to be found,
Yawning has been my only exercise
today,

Processing scented candles that have
not been lit,
Wondering how they smell as the
readymade matches laugh at my
weariness,

My skin offers comfort as I
remember how bad it was before,
Happy thoughts are interrupted by
the clicking of the fan,
Blowing medium temperature air,
I throw a loving glance at my inhaler,
and she blows me a kiss,

I hope she waits for me,
As I drag myself to her,
Like slow running maple syrup.

Disappointing Disappointments

My disappointments hang around my
neck like self-lynching,
Reaching up to my ear drums like
terrible vines whispering chants of
detention, suspension and expulsion,
Always reminding me of the dreaded
red pen making my words bleed and
hemorrhage horrifically,
Showing home movies of eyes that I
made cry,
Every tear is tallied and marked like
tattoos,
Check marks on the chalkboard next
to my name,
An endless soundtrack of melodies'
enlisting opportunities squandered,

154

Love falling and diving through the
cracks of my fingers,
One by one, each song is another's
name followed by the memory of
loving glances now gone,
Disappointment gathers like pigeons
feasting on crumbs or left-over trash,
Like self-worth and self-esteem laid
bare for the slaughter,

Ring the dinner bell,
What more Lord can disappointment
do to me,
What more do I allow,
Suddenly an earthquake in my spirit
rocks me to my knees,
No knee pads needed for their
insulated by grace,

My bravado is laced with the staccato
of my God's strength and
wonderment,
Even through the down pour from
the spirit of not good enoughism,

I suffer through, step by excruciating
step,
For I see the promised land Dr. King
talked about,
A land where these disappointments
won't nip at my heels like puppies
from hell,

156

A hell not meant for me and one I
shall never, yes, I said shall never
take up residence,
God take these chains of thorns and
vipers away from me,
I'm heavy with the rough draft of life
and the constant delete button,
Save me from myself,

Let me see what you saw when you
created me without any
disappointment in your architectural
divine creativity,
Carry me over,
Sway me through the contentment of
calm seas I long for.

Strength Echo

To see the unseeable and care for the
uncaring,
To forgive the unforgivable and pray
for those that don't pray for me,
I'm Strong,
To be grateful for the ungrateful,
To love those that hate me and not
hate those that say they love me,
To build with tools forged from fire
meant to burn me,
To tell myself how beautiful I am
when all about me screams the
opposite,
To picture myself flying amongst the
clouds with power in my wings,

158

To float across the milky way like a
shooting star,

Flapping my wings and soaring over
those that told me I could not
overcome with my dirty wings,
To hold in one pocket compassion
and in the other empathy,
To press up the mountain called Mt.
YOU NEVER WILL MAKE IT,
I run, walk, crawl and climb up the
mountain,
I will make it,

Never giving up or in,
My strength is mine.

Low Fire Burning

She once knew light as bright as
sunflowers hanging and shifting with
the Sun,
She drew with Colors of Vibrant
Vitality with Vivid Vibrations of
Victories,
She led like Moses through the
wilderness with ears still burning
from the Bush,
Yet she was replaced by a Joshua,
Little by little her light dimmed, and
the radiant sunflowers died,
The Vivacious colors she drew with
became dull and mundane,
Her memories ran on empty like a
gas tank or cereal boxes by the end of
the week,

My tears rolling down my cheek after
every visit numbered the memories I
held for her,

Memories she kept losing like pens,
socks, and winter gloves,
A revolving door, a Ferris wheel and
a merry go round of living photo
albums and home videos,
I saw these breadcrumbs flash over
and through her eyes,
comprehensive and then fleeting,

Breadcrumbs leading her home only
to be eaten by the crows of disease,

I will hold the memories for her, if I
can,

Inside my treasure chest which was
formed by her song.

Solitary Prayer

A solitary star shines best when by
itself,
Though the longing for another star
still burns,
A single willow tree sways softly in
the wind,
Though the dream of a jungle never
fails to grow,
An isolated raindrop cuts through
the air,
Though the majesty of a rainstorm
sparks the imagination,
A lone wolf runs with grace and
power,

163

Though a wolfpack exist as a force of
nature,
Help me Lord to turn you on and
turn myself off,

Lord when I feel at my lowest, you lift
me to the highest, When I am not
happy and most sad, you feel my
pain,
When I am in horrible pain and
anguish, you heal my body whole,
Lord why do you do these things for
me when I do so little for you,
Your love and support puts me to
shame,
Shame so thick and heavy that it
weighs down my heart like an
anchor,

The weight shakes my core and
buckles my knees,

Help me to love you as I should, help
me to not take your majesty for
granted,
Help me,

Even now when I feel helpless and
hopeless and unworthy,
You even now whisper in my ear how
much you love me,
You love me,
Many things are beautiful alone,
But so much more are heavenly when
together,
You love me,
So, I am plural.

165

Christmas Wordsearch

Every year my eyes search and
search,
My heart pulsates and palpitates a
pleasant and passionate percussion
laden purposeful pilgrimage,
This journey always leads to the
same place,
The same empty atmosphere of dull
pain,
Like a migraine that knows me better
than I know myself,
That pain is personal,
Christmas ornaments and wrapping
paper clutter my walk ankle deep,

166

Each step reminds me of footprints
no longer here,

Such incredible pain that screams
and bays at the moon behind my
smile,

I miss them,
All of them,
Sister's loud laughter I hear in my
memory,
But my ears do not recognize it
anymore,
Step mama is stepping up the
stairways of Heaven but wish that
she could have taken me too,

So many more, my eyes won't be able
to see,
None lock eyes back,
Every year I grow older and younger
at the same time,
Quickly becoming a part of the older
generation and not yet forty,
Quickly accepting that I am too big
for my britches sometimes,

Wishing that I could sit on someone's
lap and ask advice,
But when I look around, I see empty
couch cushions,
Plates and forks and spoons unused,
And presents left in stores,

This dull pain is grief and it pounds,
I would rather go instead of watching
others leave,
My heart sings a lonely melody but
my spirit projects with gleeful carols,
Leading me ever closer to the silent
night played by the little drummer
boy inside.

Father's Day to the Fatherless Tribe

What is Father's Day to the fatherless
tribe?
What does it mean?
Whether a father is dead, abusive,
incarcerated or absently, unlovingly
down the street, Father's Day seems
to be a reminder,
But a reminder of what?
One could say that the feeling of
rejection ascends through the
emotions and feelings of neglected
children,

170

Another might say that the currents
of anger and vengeance swells within
those who had no say so over their
mother's decision of who they would
have to call "daddy",

Still the question remains,
What is Father's Day to the fatherless
tribe?
Every year maps out the same string
of routines,
Constant commercials of smiling
boys fishing and playing catch with
heavily devoted father's,

Ever-present T.V. shows of dedicated
daddy's giving girls advice and

171

escorting them to father daughter
dances,
Endless barrages of adult son's
honoring older fathers with stories of
father son talks,
Followed by marathons of adult
daughters being walked down aisles
on wedding days,

Every year it is the same thing
replayed over and over,
Although these accounts of high
edification of father's worthy of
praise may be touching to some, but
for the fatherless tribe it's a

collection of disappointing dreams
and unrealized fantasies,

A conglomerate of envy and pain
sprinkled with should haves, would
haves and could haves,
So again, what is Father's Day to the
fatherless tribe?

The incentive of motivation and
unequaled optimism that we will be
better than our fathers,

Every Father's Day shines a light on
the greatness of fatherless sons and
the brilliance of fatherless daughters,

The fascination and unbelievable forgiveness of neglected and abused children promote character which leads to integrity,
The zeal to prove your very genealogy wrong and to proclaim in booming voices "I am not my father's actions, I am not my father's mistakes, I am not my father,
I am better than him in every way",

So, Father's Day to the Fatherless Tribe reminds us of not only who we are but more importantly who we are not,

So, for the last time, what is Father's Day to the Fatherless Tribe? A chance to plan to be what you didn't have, I hope.

The Tribe of Perseverance

We stand against the treacherous
currents, sweeping across our weary
legs,
We float while being flung towards
nearby rocks enveloped with canine
sharp edges,
Yet, we still persevere,
We are pulled down by vicious eels
that try to hold us into submission,
We fight against the torrent
tribulations of troubled waters,
Yet, we still persevere,
We walk through the wilderness
filled with sand traps, experiencing
the very antithesis of the sublime,

176

We run on hot coals till our feet

bleed from the weight of

oppression and degradation,

Yet, we still persevere,
We fly while persecuting arrows
pierce our heavenly purposed wings,
these arrows lacerate our gift of
light, but we shine on,

We sing when all about us are silent,
silent with spite, malice and envy,

Yet, we still persevere
We write with pens expressing our
thoughts and desires formed from
the beauty of our spirits and hearts,

177

While our journals and manuscripts are cast mercilessly into the flames of insecurity and contempt,

We run marathons through beds of roses while constantly being languished and lambasted by haunting hellacious thorns of tribulations,
Yet, we still persevere,
Through it all, we persevere, through it all we still hold dear the beats of our tired and true hearts, battle tested but still warring on,

178

We must not succumb neither bow to the synopsis of a storm filled night,

But persevere through the night to find the ever-present light of the never ending and enduring day,

We Persevere, We Persevere, We Persevere.

Chapter 6

Heritage of Strength

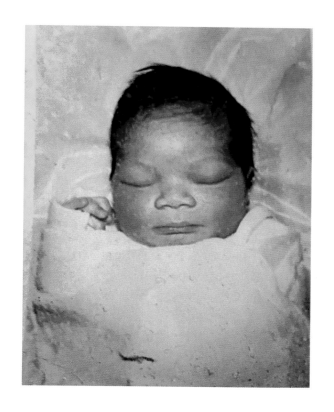

181

Freedom Floats,

Wading in persevering rivers of pain
and promise,
Piranha like chains biting around
ankles born free from wombs of
warrior queens,
Yet, these chains still won't give up,
Faces beat with oceans of salt
permeating into the scrapes and
sores from battles fought and won,
Swallowing seas of father's tears and
mother's blood under the waves,
Coming up for air only to be smacked
again by the polluted stench of ugly
hate trying to cultivate in the lungs of
strong cotton field choirs,
Passion fruit without passion forced
into the stomachs of the chosen,

182

Chosen, gifted, ordained,
They float on through it all,
Through unsinkable dominating
icebergs of hate like Mr. Jesse Owens
in Berlin,
Dolphins swim by with envious grins,

Squids clap with all tentacles as the
sharks of confusion hang their heads
in defeat,
Bite marks cannot stop freedom,
No holes can make it plummet to the
brimstone layers of hell,
Cause freedom floats,
We float.

Dear Racism

Dear racism, I'm here just as I always
was,
In your face and behind closed doors,
Down the street and around the
corner and on your front porch,
In the beginnings of your mind,
And in the back holding the torch you
thought you extinguished,
You couldn't forget about me could
you,
I won't let you,
I'm unforgettable, but you can never
run from the memory of my
greatness,

184

You cannot run from my royalty
which is why you complain,

Therefore, you hate me,
Nothing you do to trouble me with
will ever work,
For I have strength home grown,
strong as the people that came before
me,
People with backs of bricks and
heart,
You cannot see me, you never could,
I'm unbeatable,

And I will outlast you,
You will see,
Then again you won't
Cause your hate is extinguishable.

Lost Pen

Mama said I was destined for the
spotlight, that hands would clap
when eyes see me That knees would
bend to pray for me, voices would
sing to me
Now as I am on this hot pavement,
I understand what she meant
Blinded by the light of the flashlight
Documenting my movements,
Hands clapping arsenals with fingers
kissing triggers roughly,
Knees puncturing my spine, my
shoulders, my neck
Voices screaming, GET DOWN OR
DIE beating up my

eardrums like Mr. Rodney, Tears of
anger and embarrassment roll down
my cheeks

Breath kicked out of my lungs.
Forehead skin rubbed off next to the
curb, One eye surveys the regulated
footwear of my captors.
They laughed at me
They caught the big black buck on the
sidewalk.
Ready to hang my head on the wall
Then the radio sounded,
Now I am lifted in the air and the
trauma filled bracelets are taken off
Overlapping with blood and creases,
"Looks like it won't you after all boy"
"Pick your journal and your pen up"

"You aint hurt"
So, mama you were right,
I am wanted by many,
I cannot find my pen mama,
Must have rolled in the gutter along
with my naivety.

Punching Bag Got Hands

I be who I be,
I'm from where I'm from,
You best leave me be,
Before the kind me succumbs,
Cuddly with claws,
Tough with flaws,
Yes 99% teddy,
But that 1% be grizzly,
Play with me if you want.

Auction Block Prayers

Staring at a picture of me laced in
prayers and promises,
So many prayers,
Mental pictures in real time,
Five generations from slavery does
not sound that long ago,
Little baby me was prayed for with
tears in the belly of the builders of
this country,
The toilers without pay unless you
count the withdrawals of blood from
their backs,
Deposited by patty rollers or the
accounts from the auctioneer,
The only transactions they knew,

190

Yet they found time to pray for me,
Denying themselves the thought of
freedom, they poured it on me,

Whose mother was four generations
away herself,
They prayed for you too Mama,
And here I was, on the floor with
clean overalls, a bib and stainless
white socks,
Never knowing what a bullwhip felt
like,
Never having been bartered and sold
for silverware or furniture,

Never knowing the stench of the
sweaty frothy horse of the sweaty

191

frothy overseer dragging me, hand
and foot back to massa's house after

I ran all night toward the star
pointing north,
Just me sitting covered in the prayers
of freedom that I never prayed for,
I am so grateful, like an asthmatic for
air.

The Hurt is The Fight

Passion as vigorous as the blood
from the black backs painting the
rows of the cotton fields.
The screams from the slaver's tracks
deafening with despair,
Pressing on through the evil dressed
in skin not like your own,
Eyes that saw the North Star whisper
sweet everything's in your ear every
night
While Massa's promise to sell your
children if you ran yelling in your
spirit rocking your soul
You knew he was not playing

Staring at the hammer, and
horseshoe and tools made for the soil
but just perfect for the overseers'
head,

Yet you did not strike the blow,
Knowing that your man would be
castrated along with your sons,
Made to feed the same dogs that was
sent to find your brother days ago
His blood still on their hot breath as
they play,
From the hills you saw your help
coming, waiting for the true Master
to appear,
The big house was a terrible horrific
place, tip toeing around the very

194

predators the field hands could sing
about in the fields
While you were being ravaged by the
massa's sons using your private parts
as target practice to expel their
virginity

Boys and girls ushered up the steps
to be used as toys, whose private

parts were no longer private when
they were thrown off the porch
The back porch,
But you did not leave,
Why

Maybe even with all of the hellish
smells and sounds from the
plantation, there was still a veil
comfort knowing that your children,
your man, your women were with
you
Yes, father escaped, and he now is
free, but he left his wife and his
children

Now they suffer while bathing the
same dogs that ripped brother apart
Thank you for staying and proving
that we can survive even the worst
for our day is coming
Your day came because I am here

My future children's day will come
because I am here,
Rich with the knowledge and
bloodline of the unbroken
Bless all the heroes that fought but
they all fought in the way they could
By pressing like the moon against the
beautiful blackness of the night
They fought

So, God Bless you Harriet
And God Bless you unnamed black
woman who stayed and fought her
own way
I see you and you are heard.

197

Light Switch in the Dark

The North Star whispering directions
to those with captive hearts
connected to chains and blood-
stained backs,
Lighting the path through the
wilderness of the south,
The jungles of the cotton fields and
the battlefields of tobacco waves
goodbye with drooling mouths and
hate encrusted teeth with whips in
both hands,
A reminder,
Yet the North Star like the light
switch awaited our intentional
intentions to ESCAPE,
To be free,

Had to find this star amongst the
tears, pain and tree limbs weighed

down by the brothers and sisters
swinging, naked and charred,

Oh, but we found it,
Then as like now, we flip the switch
to cause the darkness to hide,
For we no longer will.

Salute the Marchers

My great grandma told me that her
mama's favorite song was based
around saints going and marching in,
I can hear and see her even now,
Just a boy watching her march like
her mama marched, now both have
long time marched in,
But what about the marchers still
here, those that marched through
trenches, sandy shores and jungles,
Through deserts and sea, through the
air, salute Tuskegee,
Warriors of sacrifice, some paying
the ultimate,

All knowing that it could have been them,

I see you,

Marching with boots to the ground making a symphonic beat matching the beat of the hearts praying for your return,
Passions and tribulations, gifts and sorrows, friends and enemies, past and future, love and loss,
All while marching,
I see you; I hear you,

Genesis to Revelation tells your tale of valor and faith,
Dear veterans I see you and I hear you marching,

She sang with fists pumping and
knees raising,
Funny how memories grab us and
reframing them tells a different and
sometimes majestic story,

Thank you for your march,
Boots traced on every cloud, on every
wave, in every sand print, through
every trench, through the wettest and
greenest jungle,
Your boot prints are appreciated,
coming in all sizes.

Harlem Hell Fighters

World War One,
Through bullets and clouds and
smoke and tears,
Courage and hope wrapped in the
prayers of those once enslaved and
chained,
History assaulted by the middle
passage and burnt by the plantations
and spit on by Jim Crow,
Fighting with courage, leaving on the
ground DNA of the brave and
uncanny resilient,
Fighting with fantastic fury and
protecting with promising purpose,
Leaving a treasured legend, never to
be forgotten,

Oh, what it must have been like to see
these hearts of honor in action,

Beating in rhythm the drum for a
country often offbeat for them,
Yet they fought
And won
And now, I write,
Thank you.

Validity Test of The Tested

The journey through the wilderness
validates our strength,
Swimming against ever persistent
currents validates our resolve,
Like hatching and learning to fly
when wings are worn and already
battle tested,
We fly anyway,
Walking on glass covered streets,
following the blood-stained
footprints of survivors long ago,
They validate me,
Forever marching, crossing finish
line after finish line after finish line,
Validation through any situation.

Swaying in the Battle Breeze

A social gathering amongst friends
and family,
Dangling and bending in the trees,
Branches and growth of bloody
blossoms,
All swaying like a choir on Sundays,
One destination and one dream,
To fight like the Ashanti and Zulu,
To fight like the brothers and sisters
at the neighboring plantation,
Or die fighting but always together,
With the butter-colored sun basting
and cooking, they rock in unison,

206

"To die fighting is to win" sings the choir from above,

"The branches know how powerful we are"
Pulling and pushing with toes at eye level,
Together is a word that terrifies those craving to divide,

But while looking up at the mighty choir,

They rock to the beat of Heaven's togetherness.

King Dreamer

A dream for the dreamers who died,
I am a dreamer through and through,
no one can hinder me,
Try? I dare you,
For I am on the road less traveled,
this straight and narrow road is
covered with gravel,
One by one I count the stones and
each pebble represents my dreams,
Not dreams deferred but dreams
preferred,
For I have seen a lot of things in my
life,
Some as fast as a bullet and some
sharp as a knife,

But I will never stop dreaming, for a
dreamer is more than a desert's oasis
but also equals many faces,

A dreamer can be a teacher, sister,
mother, brother, father or friend,
I am the son of a dreamer who
dreamed a dream that her son would
become genuine and honest,
You see dreaming is a part of me,
dating back when we dreamt to be
free,

People now say that dreamers are
losers, they say that dreams are a
waste of time,
Who are they anyway?

But what do you think this world
would be like if those bartered souls
were sleepers instead of dreamers?
What if Harriet had slept instead of
dreaming of better?
What about Frederick who
contributed more than just his
letters?
A dreamer is the architect placing
policies and changing policies and
eventually making them realities,
I will be a dreamer till the day I die,

And I wish that you would dream
with me, or I will cry,
My tears will be so my people will not
become nightmares and cold sweats
and insomniacs,

210

Please dream,
Go back to sleep in the arms of the
world that you want for yourself,
Let no one wake you up,

Dream and dream till you finish your
race,
I am a dreamer who dreams at his
own pace,
Before me there was a dream,
Before Martin there was a dream,
Before Harriet there was a dream,
I am a living dream, you are a living
dream,
Let us become dreamers and dream
to dream,
And dream to live.

Chapter 7

My Love Affair with Poetry

213

Willing Captive

I smell like poetry,
She imprinted her scent on me like
sacred tattoos or conversations from
a deathbed,
She has infiltrated my lungs to which
I only breathe her,
Like oxygen, I have grown
dependent, my dreams are colored
with her and peppered with the spice
of her voice,
My wrist and ankles are shackled
next to her,
Poetry flushed the key away a long
time ago,
Gazing in my eyes she whispers to me
without opening her mouth,

She chains herself to me and places
her forehead on mine,

No turning back now,
I enter poetry's world of fascination,
imagination, and emancipation,
I am lost in her with no desire to be
found,
These chains and shackles look good
on me,
She hums that I look good on her as
well,

Mr. And Mrs.

Pen Pregnancy

My pen flows like the falls of Niagara
sometimes,
And then it can gather like sticky
molasses and run slow,
Yet my pen can rest like someone
resting their eyes on the sky,
Waiting for the sun to come up, for a
shooting star, even waiting for love,
The inviting scroll calls for the
scribe, yet it goes to bed unsatisfied,
Hard to understand what takes so
long,
I would like to write but the precious
words seem to have evacuated my
school of creativity like children
escaping to recess,

I get worried at times, like a parent
after losing the grip of their child's
hand on Black Friday,

Where are my words?
I have something to say!
Yet my pen is still looking towards
the sky,
No Niagara, no molasses, just
looking,
It is hard to stay mad at my pen
because I love her,

Look at what she birthed, hear what
she is birthing,
Even now I'm ashamed of my
impatience,
Me and the scroll was wrong,

She was teaching us to wait, just wait
with urgency,

As she carried the babies in her
womb,
Looking to the sky was her gestation
period, fighting the word delivery,

Now I finally realize that the true
writer's block,
Was me.

The Free

Books Singing Softly,
Words Gathering Sounds from Air,
Pages Rotating.

Ink Ventriloquist

My pen speaks for me like a big
brother staring down a bully,
My pen is the candy after the bitter
cold medicine or the expresso early
in the morning,
My pen is the voice I often wished I
had hence the pen speaks for me,
Like the light speaks for the sun and
wet speaks for water,
Heat to fire, and cold to ice,
My pen spells for me,
P for Patiently
E for Expressing
And N for Nuances,

My pen presses the pages with
purpose and endless ink,
Orchestrating my heart and thoughts
into songs of poetry and reason not
always with rhymes,

But their mine,
This loquacious pen is my reflection,
my inner me, the fun house to my
amusement park,
And sometimes the house of horrors,
But always the truth,
Sometimes tasty and spinning like
slow dancing on soul train,

Skating at birthday parties and
closing my eyes imaging tires that
never flatten,

Ice that never melts or notebooks
with endless paper,
The pen speaks for me with every
papercut, ink spot and sleepless
night,

There is a song in me, and my pen
sings it,
My alter ego, my twin, my muse,
My me,
My pen is the ghost writer spilling my
words on scrolls like red Kool-Aid on
grandma's living room floor,
Intentionally proclaiming my
existence,
Keep speaking.

Knitted Words

I knit words that form the patches of
my quilt,
Covering my scars and scabs of heart
motivated wars and battles,
Rolled up over a body forged from
missions of journeys,
Hovering the breath of my former
self,
As I shake with memories so cold
that they have frostbitten the dreams
I once had,
This quilt revives even the subzero
temperatures of my anger,
Anger that pursues my joy like a
rabies laden wolf,
Not knowing why he bites,

223

Bleeding salty tears and sweating
blood,
I wrap myself inside the underbelly
of the patchy quilt,

Battle torn and scarred,
Yet warm,
As I thaw out underneath the knitted
words,
Patience calls to me,
With pencils and paper in sight,
I uncover a body riddled with love
and hate, passion and apathy and life
and death,

I reach for the pen to knit a new
patch to cover my head

224

You see,

My thoughts need comfort as well.

The Patient Empty Page

Who holds the secrets you share,
Words, sentences, and phrases
written with care,
My chest is open,
Waiting to be filled,
Through grins and tears,
Share with me what is within,
I lay here empty pondering what
your thoughts might be,
Wondering which words of truth will
set you free,
Fingertips of volcanoes about to
erupt like an angry bull,
Come and overflow and let the lava

cool,
Fill me with your truth and let the
pages decide,
My trust is what you seek,
Come give me your words to hide.

The Womb was Filled with Ink

Never was I safer than in my mama's
womb,
Knitted from head to toe,
Basking in the dreams she dreamt
for me,
Pushed out like a prince to the
slaughter,
Wet butterscotch coated with a pen
to wage war on the plantation of my
nightmares.

The Scent

The ever-present scent of the Spirit
pours through my soul and saturates
me,
My mind is cooked by the thoughts
of past rescues and forgiven sins,
My body stands on your promises
and anchored by your future
promises and by your grace,
This spirit of undying love resides in
my heart,
Full of grace and salvation,
The scent and aroma are my essence,
Like the alphabet to a poet's core.

229

Fingertips to Paper

The first time I was introduced to the
power and purity of words,
Flowing from mind, heart, soul and
spirit,
Dripping from my fingertips and
splat on the paper,
I smiled,
Understanding that what was inside
of me was as precious as the answer
YES was in aisle nine of the toy store,
"Mama please, I need that ninja
turtle, please, please, please,"
"Put it in the cart boy"
I smile,

Knowing that my thoughts needed to
be written and then verbalized,
Having the courage to express the
dreams, wants, needs and sometimes
the sufferings, makes me love myself,

I smile,
Like when I first saw my nieces and
nephews born,
I knew that my words would be
needed like gills to a fish,
Blood to a vein and hugs from this
loving uncle,

I smile,
Oh, how I love words, they
encapsulate my way of loving, my
way of giving, my way of connecting,

231

I smile,
Even when I write the word SMILE, it
feels like a commandment,
I do not have a choice, I cannot help
it,
I just smile,
Thank you for Words.

232

Revolving Door of Words

The feeling of words overlapping
through the maze of my heart,
Turning and twisting like a radio dial
or dancer,
Flowing to the right and then
learning to the left,
The words are overflowing, not
stopping but going,
Words seem lost but purposefully
driven,
Like a bus driver driving with no
route, or like a chef without a recipe,

My words of feelings and thoughts
and emotions run like river rapids
and fall like uncoordinated
snowflakes,
Some fast and some slow but they are
always moving,
My words are mine, but I do not have
to keep them,

I can control whether they stay or
not,
Either way, I am the security guard.

Hungry Pen

The loquacious pen never sleeps,
Always on duty,
Waiting to devour a devoted journal,
Never gets full,
But is insatiable,
Leaving words with intentionality,
Like footprints dripping with ink.

The Word Army

Here they come,
With sword like pens in one hand
and ink in the other,
Ready for battle with shields of
journals and arrows of paper,
Fighting the ills of the spirit and
warring against the ever present
confused laced writers block of
comparisons,
The antithesis of self-worth,
Yet we march with shoes laced tight
and hearts beating the percussion of
the rallying cry,
No more shutting eyes pretending to
be sleep, no, no, no,

Now we fortify our words with love
dripping resiliency
like a solitary star in the sky or lily
amongst the weeds,

We are here,
Journals waiting to be fed.

Every Snap at a Spoken Word

Flying down with a P on our chest,
O for Overflowing,
E for Essentially,
T for Trustworthy,
P-O-E-T, we be the poets,
Swooping down and saving babies
and rescuing cats,
Yes, all of that,
With pens from on high we vanquish
tormentors that torment souls,
Treating these souls with anointed
ointment used for deep cleansing,
Precious tears we catch with steady
hands cradled in cup shapes made
for restoring,
Reviving the dead and thumping
willing hearts to beat again,

Kissing the lips of those never been
kissed,
Holding necks and wrapping minds
in warm comforting knots like tight
shoelaces,
Patching up emotions raw like turnip
greens and onions, calling tears that
were once dried,
With damp journals laced with
blood, guts and moisture from
moments of holding things in,

Yes, we go through it,
We are the billboards for others to
see and read and be read to,
To outline dreams, and interpret
them,

To spell out trauma like a third-grade
spelling bee, when letters cannot be
found,
To be the lifeguard not allowing one
to drown in the sweat of a nightmare,
We be the poets,
Flying with pens in hand and P on
our chest,

Overflowing essential and
trustworthy,

240

Saving lives with every snap of
fingers of those locked in fiery
furnaces,

Still daring to breathe through the
smoke,
We be the poets, with P on our
chests,
Snap, snap, snap, snap, a new poet
gets their pen,
Like angels to wings.

Prayer Precious Prayer

Letter to Heaven like seconds to
minutes,
No carrier pigeons or express jets
needed,
Just faithful appreciation to ears that
never slumber,
Anticipating answers for years
scarred and wilted,
Tears that flow upstream, not down,
Like a ladder that pain climbs just to
be heard,

Grandma said to pray before things became lost,
Great grandma said to pray to move forward,
Precious.

Poetry by Lantern Light

As I sit here thinking of what to pen,
I'm startled by the thoughts of where
I have been,
Times of unspeakable precious joys
and then fears,
Memories of laughter and epiphanies
and moments of tears,
Tears so deep that a ship could find
passage,
So much unpacking left to do with all
this baggage,
The reality is I know all too well
about rejection,
Top to bottom as long as a funeral
procession,

But as I sit pen in hand next to the lantern,
I realize that my pen has been my companion,

Lantern light providing the perfect light and shadows,

Making it easy to dodge the gallows.

Moon Dancer

The pencil twisting,
Singing letters loudly,
Heard under the moon,
Deciphered throughout the Heavens,
The eraser plays redeeming
melodies,
Humming and sawing away vowels
and snapping consonants,
The loose-leaf paper eating words
like midnight snacks.

We are Here

Like currents of life in a sea of chaos,
yet we are here,
Like seaweed entangled by pain and
pleasure, tragedy and triumphs,
scars and sacrifices,
But through it all, we are here,
Like honey dripping from the stinger
of a bee,
Lava pouring out of a once tamed
volcano,
We are here,
Stretching our arms and grabbing
the fabric of a quilt made of peace,
Knitting our hearts with the
embroidery of the resilient, the
humble, the compassionate,

247

Now we are here,

Punching through the fog that
envelopes like weighted blankets,
waiting for my suffocation,
Kicking through the fog like the heat
from fire, waiting for my burning,
Journaling our journey, but not
alone
But with pen and pad, pencil and
notebook, keys and laptop,
We are here, we are here, we are
here,

Together.

248

My Journal Keyed My Car

So, my journal is mad at me,
Talking about, I'm cheating on her,
She said my words fit her pages like
DNA and fingerprints,
Yet I gave my words to the laptop,
I cried and begged like Mr. Ruffin,
Got on bended knee because she's
been a rider since I was a boy to man,
The roll over is what I'm getting,
Emotional affairs she whispers,
Gonna be a long night,
She be scary,
I yearned all day to fill her pages,

But not tonight she said,
I knew that laptop was trouble, but
her keys were just right,
Now banished to the couch,
Swollen with syllables, similes,
metaphors and analogies,
Betrayed by my words,
The laptop was winking at me from
the screen like Potiphar's wife.

Wayward Pen

She moves with the grace of an angel
but there is a demon underneath,
Her face is as radiant and bright as
the sun but behind that face exist
only darkness,
The touch from her feels as soft as a
cloud but that touch leaves behind
cuts and bruises,
The pleasant, sweet, and loving
aroma of her is intoxicating but the
pleasant, sweet, and loving aroma is
poisonous gas,

Eyes sparkling with truth and
honesty, but the gaze from those eyes
hide lies and schemes,
A smile so glorious that it seemed
Heaven sent but this smile can only
be from the pits of hell,

The sound of her voice is like a
thousand symphonies, but
underneath this score lives evil
hidden messages,
Her hatred for me is marked by
conditional love,
Woe is me; Woe is me,
For I know who and what she is,
She moves with the grace of an angel,

And her hate is masked by
conditional love,
Why did I even notice her?
I should have kept walking.

Respite

My words not flowing tonight,
Thoughts caught in a net,
Feelings behind a dam laced with
fatigue,
Emotions struggling in a spider web,
Pen is asleep,
But there is extra ink spotting the
page,
So, I connect the dots of the
remnants of creativity, Coloring in
between the lines with whatever
colors are left,
Constipation in my fingers,
Pen tossing in dreamland,

I shake her but her eyes stay closed,
So, these leftover ink crumbs are all I
have to feed this page.

En Fuego

Someone asked me how can I write
the way I do,
My answer was and is the following:
"I am programmed that way"
Like a terminator of cramped fingers
and writer's block,
I move like the wind through the
thesaurus of my upmost thoughts,
There lies a delicate aroma of
passion that leads to pain that circles
back to passion again,
Over and over and over again,
I get sick to my stomach trying to
keep down all these words,
They are so heavy,

256

Sometimes I can barely stand
because the weight of
analogies and metaphors smothering
me,

My pen pens with penmanship the
pinnacle of promise so soft that you
can hear a pin drop,

I am punctured by words,
I hear words that have not been
invented and I hear words that have
been forgotten,
My heart holds the treasure chest of
those pen wielders and yielders that
came before me,

I hear with every syllable the rapture
of words,

I write this way because I am on fire,
en fuego for words,
They crave and scream to be
released,
And I hold the key to their freedom,
I possess the combination to the
conjunction between dungeon and
daylight,
And, but, yet, however, although
firstly and lastly all find the genesis
from the ballpoint of my pen,
I'm a fire poet because I was made in
the fiery furnace,
My hands and fingertips molded by
the Blacksmith of all blacksmiths,

Constructed to bring forth letters
that are countless like the count of a
zillion hummingbird wings,

258

Pulsating the air,
My pen is ordained,
My pen is beautiful,
My pen sets me ablaze,

I am burned and scorched with
words,
Fire, brimstone and poetry I be.

Always Poetry I Be

I Love My Skin Deep

I would be the sexiest man in the
world if my words were my skin,
Walk into any room and drain it with
every syllable and synonym,
The beauty of the skin connects to
ancestors here and gone, earth to
sun,
With tales of courage, love and fight,
rivers of letters run down over my
head,
Coating my head like grease before
Sunday school,
Born to a queen, and mama didn't
write no fool,

But what if my words really were my skin,
Would loving me matter if you already read what was within?

Pen Pillow Talk

My pen was talking again this
morning,
Whispering sweet everything's in my
ear,
Nibbling my lobes,
Passionately drawing blueprints of
metaphors on my back,
Kissing me incessantly with the
double entendre of entourages of
themes and schemes,
They flow like moonbeams through
our movie role playing scenes,
I must get up and satisfy the
insatiable pen,

The pen calls my name even when
there is no paper in sight,
She is my might,

When all I can see is unyielding
night.

Poetry Cupid

Every line of the page marks the
minutes I want to spend with you,
The syllables used envelopes the
seconds that tease me,
Like bullets kissing me,
Riddling my chest with long suffering
touches,
Long lasting, long winded and
longing looks of fascination,
You stamped words on my love
outlined by a body used to transport
the words you blew my way,
Like sweet pound cake with lemon
icing,

You fit and complete just right,
Sweet and tart like kissing and biting,
You keep leaving marks on me,

Your ink is darker than my melanin,
Everyone can see the remnants of
our times together,
I be a poet,
No more hiding our hearts that beat
in unison the fabric of love,
Poetry you are no longer my secret
lover,

To the mountain tops I get down on
one knee,
The ring of reason, rhythm and
rhyme I place on your finger,

265

As you dart my eyes with letters of
pain,
Hope and decay are all wrapped
together beautifully,
Giving me my life no longer unheard,
You shot me last night with bullets of
bars and stanzas,
Kissing me and I liked it.

Acronymic Poetic Love Affair

PURITY
of love capsizing my fears and gifting
me my desires,
OPENLY
caressing and performing heat
rituals caramelizing my inner being,
EVAPORATED
sweat pouring from pores left ajar
seeking refuge inside your warm
honeycombs again,
TANTALIZING
titillations tickling my voice once told
to shut up,
ROUTING

and rerouting in the blossoms of
your bosom of essence, soft and
saturated,
YOU
are what makes my motivation worth
longing for, foreplay with every
stroke of my pen,

My not so secret yet secret love affair,
Thank you for every ink lip mark on
my neck,
POETRY.

Poet's Chair

We are all poets,
But just a few of us know it,
Rocking pens easy like chairs,
Ink gathering like open ears and
stares,
You listen because you must,
Pens are always wet, leaves no rust.

Chapter 8

Stigma less Mental Health

271

Therapy in the Shadows

There were many sunrises that I wish
would never have risen,
There were many stars in the sky that
I wished would have fallen out of
sight,
Every mirror I saw I wanted to burst
and crack.
I wanted to unhook myself from this
world and everything in it,
I hated me so bad that it made me
mad looking at others
Wishing that I would not have to live
having to hear over and over and
over and over how blessed I was,
How beautiful I was, how wonderful
I was and never seeing it for myself,

I need internal glasses to see what
people claim they saw in me and yet I
always felt invisible,
Despite whom talked to me despite
the eyeballs on me despite how many
heard my voice,
I still felt like air that floats in and
out of rooms around and through
people,

Up and down, left and right, diagonal
to the point and oftentimes
mercurial,
I wanted to be seen so bad, but my
shyness would not allow me to speak
loudly,
I wanted the spotlight, but my low
self-esteem kept me in the shadows
that marked death for me,

273

And I was cool with that,
Death seemed like a welcomed
friend, a friend coming to see me,
coming to chill with me, that
understood me
Oh, how I hated what I had become,
I wished the sun had stayed in
perpetual darkness,

I wish the stars had burned out all
because of the hatred that I had for
me
But I was fearfully and wonderfully
made, I am God's child and yet my
twisted mind wouldn't let me see it,
What I did see were all those pill
bottles I had filled with what I felt
were little capsules of truth,

It

spelled out the funeral home name,
I wrote NO on my left hand,
And
I wrote DON'T on my right hand just
to remind myself not to eat these
capsules,
NO, DON'T
NO, DON'T
NO, DON'T
Well, I did not
I am still here fighting against those
thoughts, day by day
Understanding that going the
distance must count for something,

Now I wait and look for the sun,

Now I look and I connect the dots of
all the stars searching for the north
star to lead me home,
I am fearfully and wonderfully made;
I know that now as I knew then but
something different happened,
A change happened,
A dream,

An epiphany,
A vision
Now I stand here asking for
forgiveness,
I am also asking for mercy,
I want to see what others see in me,
I want to know why I never believed
them,

That answer I already know but one
thing is for certain,

Those capsules did not dictate my
fate,
My mind was not in charge,
My body was built and made to be
destroyed,
Rebuilt, destroyed, and rebuilt again,
That is all I know,
And you know what,
I am a superhero
A man who breaks and comes back
together,
I stand in the furnace,
And I am so glad that someone is in
there with me,

Because I was fearfully and
wonderfully made,
Those pills spelling my death,

are not my God.

Therapy is the tool that He gave me,
And it sharpens me,
Allowing me to shine like mamas
hope for me,
I fell out of the womb with tools
honed and rehearsed on the couch.

278

Therapy Treat

Therapy Baby,
Masking and Unmasking Me,
It's True, Me be Free

9-8-8 Truth Serum

"Hello, Hello, Hey,
I need help but I do not know how to
ask or what to ask for,
I am not sure what is wrong or even
what I expect from this call,
But
Help me please,
I smiled all day today and laughed so
hard that I cried,
And yet I still dialed these three
numbers,
The wrinkles in the corners of my
eyes when I smile now resemble cuts
deep within the earth's crust,

Teeming with seas of trauma soft
tears,
Like melt away peppermints,
All colors are dimmed, and all voices
seem far away like the last time I was
genuinely happy,

I am tired and alone even when
surrounded by faces who say they
love me,
The warmth of their love antagonizes
me,
Why am I so unhappy when everyone
constantly tells me how happy I
should be?

Can you help me?"

Sometimes Positivity Can Stink

I know you miss your sister boy, but
you will get over it,
Oh, I am sorry your husband cheated
maam, but stop all that crying cause
they all do,
You know if you worry, have doubt,
get nervous, that you are questioning
God, right?
Shhh best keep your feelings to
yourself and smile more,
In fact, stomp on your feelings,
unless you want to remain unfaithful
and ungrateful,
Just be happy for a change, you act
like you the only one that lost a job
before,

Hey, I had a bully in school to, you
not special,

Just smile and laugh it off,
Your tears are fears, did you know
that?
So, what, at least you have other
children, it is time to stop mourning
this one in the grave, he is
in Heaven,
"HELP ME",
Toxic Positivity has been forced fed
down my throat like sweet smelling
cough medicine that
never really stops the cough,
Just ignores it for a little while,

It suppresses my emotions, my
thoughts, my memories, my self-
importance, my life,
Tries to bend and shape shift me to
fit a mold of a robot,

One I was never meant to be,
When I am down, I try to climb up
but some days, like today,
I need a hand to hold while I am in
the valley,
Stop jerking my arm out of socket
before I am ready,
Allow me a chance to feel,
Allow me a chance to grow,
Allow me to feel the weeds that choke
me,
And allow me to talk about it,

284

For that is the real reason you want
me to act happy,
Cause you don't actually want to
support,
Do you?
You just want me to shut up and be
happy so I can stop making you feel
like a rash under your

arms,
Uncomfortable,
It is hard work loving someone who
hurts,
But I am sorry that it makes you
nervous,
I miss my sister, I cry all the time,
I often feel lost without her,
You say for me to deal with it,

All the spouses that have cheated has
nothing to do with her husband,
Create space to heal and let her cry
and or fuss if she wants,
Just stop telling people that what
they feel is wrong,

Express that using positive thoughts
are helpful but another side must
exist as well.

Therapy Session

Muscles tightening, eyes tearing, toes
tapping, and hearts thumping,
Storytelling, ears listening, clock
ticking and notes taking,
Hearts breaking, hearts mending,
hearts talking and hearts aching,
Empathy giving, sympathy giving,
ears giving, smiles giving,
Cheeks reddening, noses dripping,
fingers scratching and bladders
holding,
Memories recounting, memories
making, memories processing,
memories expressing,
Pores pouring, bodies stirring,
knuckles popping and heads hurting,

287

Self-caring, motivation sharing,
acceptance accepting and
compassion blending,
The sandy beach like client and the
calming weather-like therapist,
meeting each other with purpose,
Pulling and pushing, wandering, and
wondering,
Hoping, and helping,
Until next time and the cycle begins
again,

Hopefully on time.

Whisper from Below

Suicidal thoughts consume like a
wildfire does,
Red life flows from ready veins,
Waiting to burst over,
Quicksand suffocating with blades,
Time to check that whisper,
Make the Exodus from the
Quicksand,
If I fall, the blade falls,
Blades are too sharp to leave on the
floor.

Closed and Under-Construction

I'm a good man,
Cause I said so,
Fought battles not my own
constantly,
Like arrows cutting through my
peace,
And yet I bleed blood even before I'm
cut,
Knees puffed praying prayers not
meant for me,
My chest big like a volcano splashing
lava back in my face,
Skin melting off my skull erasing my
painted-on smile,
I'm just a clown crying tears no one
cares to help me wipe,

It's time to my take cape off,
It doesn't fit no more,
Time to hibernate like the

teddy I am,

But,
I am a good man and yes, I did need
to say it.

Resurrection Inspiration

How can one resurrect the parts that
have been murdered by others,
Parts that you hold special and
unique,
Parts that are yours,
Parts that make you fearfully and
wonderfully made,
And they stole them from you,
Hid them from you,
Killed them in front of you,
Oh, but today it is time like the bell
on an oven or earliest bird chirping
outside the window,
It is time for resurrection,
Time to roll back the stones locking
you up with doubt and distortions,

Time to get up,

**Time to rise and be who you were
created to be,
It is time to ascend.**

293

Beat Up

Yo, depression is a silent monster,
Smiling at the mirror, making deals
with my countenance,
Cutting me at the ankles and tickling
my inner bully that laughs at myself,
Ferociously,
Leaving sasquatch sized footprints
across my chest creeping in my
bloodstream the poison of weeds and
thorns,
Hugging relentlessly to me like vines
through an unkempt gate,
Causing a rattle when I walk like the
tail of a snake
chiming wind songs of despair,

Like a plant escaping the insulation
of a seed fighting through the soil,
Swimming in the pot God put me in,
Breaching the surface,
Trying my best to kiss with sun
scorched lips,
But,
That monster keeps punching and
busting my lips and restructuring my
jawline,

Like a whack a mole, I keep getting
hit,
Choke slammed and twisting my
arm, trying to make me scream
uncle,

But "I can't behave",
Never knew how,
I go the distance, getting back up
repeatedly, like Rocky,
Broken and bloody, teeth and tears
missing but I can't behave,
Declining confidence singing my
name as sweet as Gladys and
powerful as Maya's words,
But I can't behave,
Depression, you won this round, but
I didn't go down,
My legs are still moving and my heart
still singing the war cry of the
kingdom,

**Fighting to continue to slay this
monster,
With tears staining both cheeks and
flirting with the sun.**

Scared of Fear, Scared of Me

I scare me, I make myself shake like
the earth does when it adjusts itself,
I scare me when I shift my own
atmosphere and climb mountains of
my own,
I scare me, like the dark used to and
the haunting anxiety of a chalk board
with my name on it,
Looming and staring at me,
I scare me when I try to fly but I have
no wings, when I try to talk without a
tongue,
When I try to love but my heart beats
offbeat,

298

I scare me so much,
Fear grips so tight that it is a
constant companion,
So connected and consistent that it
appears loving,

Yet this fear that scares me has an
expiration date, like NOW,
I do not want to be afraid of myself, I
want to love myself like the first look
through the eyes of a newborn,

Like the dry earth feels after the first
new raindrop,

Praying and affirmations are needed
to overcome my fear,
My heartbreak,
My soul fracture,
God's love must save me and cool the
flames while igniting the frost that
haunts the window of my heart,
Yet still I will overcome, I refuse any
other option,

I scare me, but not for long,
I choose to love me harder and scare
the fear inside of me, OUT,
Away and flee from me,
NOW.

I Am Okay

Swimming through the air,
Flying through the sea,
Laughing with tears,
Crying through giggles,
Nothing about this pain makes sense
right now,
Nothing about what I'm feeling
seems real,
Except from these tear-stained
cheeks,
And my hands outstretched to the
sky,
Waiting for answers,

All that is known is my love was real,
Still real,
In that,
I am content to swim through the air,
Fly through the sea,

Laugh through my tears and cry
through my giggles,

I AM OKAY,
And that is good enough for now.

Dichotomy of Thoughts

PTSD,
God, I wish I knew which thought
takes priority,
Like the first raindrop released from
the heavens,
Or,
The first formation of a cloud that
calls the attention of the eyes that
gaze upon it,
All I know is that I have thoughts like
these,
Random thoughts,
Thoughts that encompass dreams as
big as the universe that nestles the
earth,

And wide as the imagination I held as
a child,
So many thoughts of tragedy I have
wrapped with past trauma and yet
there is hope,

Like the beauty of a rose trapped
beneath and amongst weeds and
thorns,
My tragedies and trauma cannot hide
my triumphs,
They appear and disappear at the
same time,
But,

I know they are there present like the
arms of love holding me and keeping
me warm,
Fireplace of contentment,

304

God above, will these thoughts ever
quiet down?
Will they slow down, should I even
want them too,
Like a never-ending photo album of
trials and tribulations like my mama
talked about,
But there is triumph and
thanksgiving there too,

Lord my thoughts have lied to me,
They have pretended to be plural,
like a couple or team,
But they are really one,
One constant, one singular cloud
forever covering the light of the sun
that is in me,

What do I do with these thoughts?
What can I do about it?
This thought screams at me
sometimes like an angry jaguar,
Then it whispers like a persistent
mosquito,
But always saying the same thing,
"It is your fault, and you are not good
enough"

Please do something God about this
thought,
So present that it sounds comforting
like the serpent from Eden,
I do not want to bite the apple,
But it looks so delicious like sweet
potato pie and collard greens,

Please vacuum this lying conniving
thought from my mind,
Find the stench lingering in my heart
and the shadow of it on my spirit,
Remove, remove, remove,
I want to be alive,
No longer sleep.

307

Bulldozer

What blooms from a mind full of
mine fields,
Explosions of emotion and
thoughtful distortions highlighting
my mind's urgency,
Emergencies populated by sirens and
screams,
Infectious soundtracks and
swimming through ideations and
diagnostics,
What can bloom from a mind like
this,
Crying to be heard and breaking to be
resurrected,
A weed garden up there,

308

Full of thorns and prickly bushes,
What blooms are huge mushrooms,
Hanging like umbrellas of traumatic
will in testaments,

It's time to fire my inner gardener
and hire the bulldozer,
Come evacuate the mine field with
haste,

Let me find the blueprint

to the green pastures and

still waters King David wrote about,

That's the blossoming I want to
retreat to.

309

Train Trip of Thoughts

On a train, crossing state lines, over
tracks glazed by the rain,
Peering through wide window blinds,
allowing me to view landscapes of all
kinds,
Hearing the clicks of the tracks below
my feet, as I keep score as the sights
and wonders I see compete,
Not knowing what I'm chasing, or
what chases me, knowing I must go
back but for now, I'm happy to be
free,

Free to think or not to think,
replaying memories of my choosing,
refocusing with every blink,
The whistle blowing across the air,
with the rattle of food carts carrying
food wrapped with care,

My body swaying to the vibrant
vibrations, moving over canyons of
puzzles and proclamations,
Snowflakes and sun,
Heat and cold,
The green of nature,
The color of the desert,
All seem near yet distant,

And I'm alone because I want to be,

With thoughts laid open and heart
rejuvenating with the tracks so
consistent,
Disconnected from connections and
de-escalating from escalations, the
train carries me in revelations with
resuscitations,
As the Choo Choo plays the lullabies,
I'm lulled to sleep by the conductor's
soundtrack,

Dreaming of inspiration and rest,
taught to me on the railroad track.

OCD Rerun

I did it again,
Repeating the word amen so much
that I forgot what I was praying for,
Throwing trash in the trashcan and
reaching inside over and over
because the paper towel did not land
where it should have,
Trying to make myself cry more
because the right side of my cheek
was wetter than the left,
My left tear duct needed to catch up,
Going through full deodorants in
half a week, got to have 27 wipes per
arm or else,

Uh oh, I scratched my itchy right thumb, it's time to scratch my non itching left thumb, just to be safe,

Jesus help me, my pillow fell on the floor and now I cannot sleep on it tonight,
I stayed in the bathroom for an hour at the mall with friends waiting for me yesterday,
I was done but there were no paper towels, so I could not open the door to leave,

I did not want to buy this, but I touched it already, so I have too,

Did I tap my right knee 14 times
today or 13,
Will she die if I do not pray again,
Sinner's prayer verbatim, over and
over and over and over and over,

Wrong sequence, sinner's prayer
verbatim again, over and over and
over again,
Mama I cannot move through this
aisle until I finish this prayer,
Jesus help me,
Lord have mercy, I forgot to say in
Jesus' name,

315

33 more sinner's prayers, Jesus was
33 when He went to the cross right?

Over and over, louder and louder,
Intrusive thoughts before I knew
how to spell them,
Over and over, louder and louder,
Sinner's prayer time again,
While I count random gas station
receipts from 15 years ago
I just cannot throw them away,
Just like these thoughts,

Over and over,
I am so over it,

Prayer works but it is okay to pray
for better mental health,
Over and over,
Amen...

Job Description

Wiping blood-stained cheeks from
tears and broken spirits,
Bruised souls with cracks wide and
deep,
Decapitated minds and battered
dreams,
Elevated stress reaped long ago,
Incarcerated thoughts overlapping,
over and over,
Punctures and stabs,
Sacred thoughts scarred,
And yet we still give them
understanding,

318

We point out redemption and
resilience,
We show compassion and empathy,
No matter what, we serve as servant
soldiers,

Doing the work that leads to life and
medicates with the enduring salve of
therapy.

Dear Appointment

Having the beat and fabric of drums
and blankets,
Swaying to the rhythm of a zillion
songs of hurt and hope,
Staying warm under the knitted
covers of goals and growth,
With clouds of imagination and
mountains to realize,
With pens of thought and journals
overflowing,
Poems and passages trickling from
scarred hearts,

Dripping down life's resume and
stained with honest tears,
Client to therapist, like water to sea,
Unlocking and paroling incarcerated
ideas and dreams,

Uncovering misused mirrors and
invisible reflections, Building new
mirrors and highlighting true
reflections,

Fashioned with wings now, flying
with purpose now,

321

**Tackling the untacklable while
enjoying the stream of peace, cooling
my wounds.**

Costume Treats and Cognitive Tricks

Every year I put on the same
costume,
Made of invisible dirty shouldas,
Cold couldas and wet wouldas,
All masked and draped with smiles
and cheers,
Boots laced with insecurities and
buttons of trauma debris,
Yet no one can see because of my
costume,
The helper who doesn't need help,
Wanderer who is tired of wondering
why wandering matters,
Fastening and fashioning my
costume ready for sugarless

treats and tricks that often leave me
rotting,

Like old pumpkins I can get mushy,
But my formed fitting costume never
rips, always stitched tight,
Knitted so well that it seems to be all
of me,
And that's the real trick,
And the real problem,
Difficult to chew and get rid of like
stale candy corn and salty honesty.

324

The Steps to Stepping

Processing the loss of what it all
means can be tough,
Tough like Papa was before he
crossed river Jordan,
Processing where do we go from here
can be rough,
Rough like the stories of Grandma's
childhood,
Processing how we should feel is
confusing,
Confusing like geometry class was,
never finding the right angle,
Family,
So much goes into the word,
Like a small beehive with a thousand
bees inside you cannot see,

Maybe we do not have to know how
to process,
Maybe we can just be,

And let the process flow like the
honey from the hive,
Slow and rich and right when it hits
the dirt below,
With purpose, thickness and
sweetness.

Silent Drummer of Mental Abuse

Stop playing percussion on my
mama,
I'm done hearing that drum solo,
The symbol of cymbals being played
and replayed haunts me,
I can hear every down beat and every
upbeat,
Like the snare you snared her, not
wanting to release,
Your hands like the sticks, over and
over, never out of synch,
The kick stand was assembled as you
kicked and then stood over her,
Stop it, stop it, stop it, I can still hear
me screaming, harmonizing with her
chorus,

You are the worst kind of drummer,
for you are a hope stealing
conductor,

Swaying and bending notes full of
grunts, whimpers and hollers,
lubricated by blood and tears,
Yet she outlasted you didn't she,
She rose while you fell didn't she,

328

A face once full of woeful tears, now
shines with evergreen tears of joy,

Now your masterpiece of percussion
is the soundtrack of your failed
concert,
You couldn't beat it out of her, your
sticks of mental weaponry were too
brittle,
But I wish you well anyway,
So, I can move through.

Yesterday and Today's Lady

The life she lived flowed up stream
not down,
Sun radiated coldness kissing the
ground,
And the wind never blew,
This lady stayed up late,
Counting the memories of her
escape,
Retelling beautiful races wrapped in
yesterday,
Wincing at scary faces marking her
decay,
Yet what stories did she hold,
How many secrets yet to unfold,
She sat with her face pressed against
her window,

Always searching for her love never
remembering she was a widow,
Forced to relive the life she lived
decades ago,

Barely remembering today's dinner
or the lunch before,

The life she lived had dry oceans,
Moon and stars were unplugged at
night,
And one pair of eyes felt like a
thousand gazes of percussion,

This lady never knew why,
Her memories ran on empty,
Tender yet a fading supply.

331

Integumentary

I hurt too under this skin,
My epidermis is pierced, and the
dermis ravaged,
Forced to carry weight not my own,
While filtrating the guilt of carrying
it,
Feet burnt while walking on hot coals
lit by the matches of others,
As self-sabotage stabs my inner core
with almosts and maybes,
I'm rashy and irritated,
Allergic to meanness, yes meanness,
Makes me itch,

332

Self-disclosure can be the self-care
salve for my wounds,
Yet I might be running out of it,

Seasons change like the texture of my
integumentary,
A system made from God but torn up
by the opposite,
I hurt too under this skin,
Not bullet proof nor immune to
bullies of the heart,
Infecting my mind with the purpose
of making me feel purposeless.

Maybe I left too early

I received a love letter today,

The cave that once housed me in dampness and decay, wrote to say hey,

The ravenous force of nature roared at me from the penmanship of hieroglyphics,

Matched with intense calligraphy that only I can read,

Decipher and decode,

I fought so hard to be out of its grasps,

334

Broke out chasing freedom but freedom is not what I dreamed it would be,

Now with freedom all around I find it easy to fall prey,

Preying on me are superior minds that pick on mine,

It is hard for me to keep up, "I do not know what yall talking about",

I pray not to be prey, but I am left in the open on this prairie,

The letter passionately requests me to go back to where things made sense,

335

In the sinkholes of life that I became
accustomed to,

Where I did not need to shield my
eyes from the rays of the great star by
day,

Nor the pale light of the dusty sphere
that appears at night,

I could just sit and be,

Not bothering anyone, not hurting
anyone, not cause one dismay nor
confusion,

I get in trouble being away from the
cave and it knows it,

How did it get my address, how did it
smell my anxiety,

How did it know that my
awkwardness would be heavy like an
Angelou poem or as strong and
devastating as Otis Redding octaves,

The darkness of the cave is where I do not have to apologize nor be disappointed,

For there is no one else to say I'm sorry to, just me, just me, just me,

The cave left its scent on the letter,

Smells like me, underneath the weighted blanket of time and my missed prime.

Feels Go the Dynamite

Here I am drowning in a black hole,
No sound when I scream,
Not even sight across the stillness of
the other side of the moon,
And yet the presence of my own
hands around my neck is visible,
The heat from the middle of my
forefinger and thumb is
recognizable,
The wetness of sweat from the palm
pushing against my windpipe feels
like currents of hate,
Self-hate,

How did I get here,
How do I get out,
I blink " rescue me" like Morse Code,

Yet I'm losing, wheezing, sinking,

Why is it so absent here,
Thick like petroleum jelly
encapsulating my thoughts,
Rendering the smell of me odorless,
No one sees me, no one smells me, no
one can find me,
Still sinking with my own hand
squeezing ever tighter.

340

Strength Don't Mean Painless

Who hears their own thoughts?
Who thinks about their thoughts?
Who takes time to feel and massage
feelings forged and fried long ago?
Who knows them well enough to let
them go like doves at a gravesite?
When will we understand that we
were fearfully and wonderfully
made?
Not robots made on an assembly line,
Yes you, you hurt too,
No artificial intelligence and no
motor oil,
But blood, flesh and heartbeats,
Stop playing like your body, spirit
and mind don't get bruised,

341

Stop playing that you don't cry at
night,
In the bed, on the road, brushing
your teeth and in prayer,
Your tears have tears,
Why won't you admit that you have
pain,
Pain masked by "I'm alrights and I
don't cares"

You are not alright, and you do care,

Acknowledging doesn't take away
your strength,
It allows you to be there for yourself,
To hold yourself with arms that fit
your twists and turns,
So, tell the truth, You hurt too,
Let's find the medicine that can help,

342

The prescription of self-love and
honesty,
X-ray glasses to find and evacuate the
monsters hidden within thoughts,
feelings and behaviors,
So, why do we lie?

Sessions of Cotton

From the smothering cotton fields,
toiling under the unforgiving sun,
Hands bleeding and backs hurting
with the beads of sweat pouring like
fountains,
Feet holding endless soul shattering
pain matched with eyes darkened
with mind numbing work,
Can you see their thoughts? Can you
see yours?
Minds focused on children, some
running underfoot, some working
and toiling alongside mothers and
fathers, only held together by the
brokenness of hearts faintly beating,
Help, justice, help,

Where are the dreams, where are the goals, where is the hope?

Dreaming dreams and wishing wishes of future realities

Only to be interrupted by the cramps and growls of stomachs on empty, Married to parched tongues and throats like sand,

Limping with crooked legs barely supporting backs broken and twisted, mirroring question marks, Who can they talk to? Who even cared to listen?

345

But you have us, and we have you, we
care here,
We see the souls soaring through the
smothering cottonfields of life,
You flow through the unforgiven sun,
but here you will find forgiveness
and acceptance,
You run through the bleeding hands
and hurting backs but here those
hands will be held, and the backs
supported,

You walked with feet encapsulated by
endless soul shattering pain, but
here you will be carried,

346

You saw through poorly lit eyes, but
here light will light your path,
You spoke through parched tongues
and throats of sand, but here your
voices will be heard and comforted,
You journeyed with legs and backs
weary, frightful and angry, but here
you will not walk alone,

There is hope for the hurting, there is
hope here.

Pick Up and Delivery

Pack up this feeling of not good
enough and send it on its way,
I'm also done with the thoughts of
perfectionism darkening my
doorway, take that today,
Oh, and leaning against the door is
the self-hating box,
You can take that too, tired of those
stumbling blocks,
Don't care how you load them in the
truck,
Just make sure they don't get stuck,
Stuck here that is,
Now be delicate with my peace,
Deliver that with care,
Unload with purpose with

348

patience to share,

In fact, give me those boxes marked
patience, and give me that
encouragement letter to fight my
complacence,
I need more self-worth, please go
back and get more, and bring
laughter as well,
So much you can't fit it through the
door.

Now Sit in It

Can others see what I see,
Evaporating tragedy after tragedy
just to be me,
Pressing through and pushing
through only to be pulled through,
Pulled like the North Star where
freedom was found for a few,
Focusing on what is noble like Isaiah
32:8,
Working on what is present and what
is currently on my plate,
It's too hard to think too far in the
future,
I'm trying to decrease my worry,
Too many twists and maybes too
many burdens to carry,

350

So, I try to stick and sit in my
accomplishments,

Working on second by second to
improve and never shying from
compliments,
I wonder if people see what I see,
Or should I even wonder,
Maybe I will start appreciating me
for a change,
Through the sunlight and thunder.

Stop Kissing Me

This mosquito thinks she goes with
me,
All this whispering in my ear every
night, it's starting to get to me,
I can't shake her, all night long,
Turning on the light does nothing,
she just stares and rubs her hands
together,
Winking at me, all flush with red,
Yo, I declare I don't want you like
that,
Waving my arms just makes her
come closer with honeymoon
intentions and blood thirst,

Next time I gotta be quicker with that
screen door,
You are not a gold digger but a blood
miner,

I need mine more than you want
mine,
Let me sleep please, I aint yo man,
But at least you are persistent in a
cute way, I do like that,
But c'mon now,
Nevermind, got no time to argue,
Just stop talking and go to sleep,
I gotta work in a few hours,
Thief.

Surrogate Coins

I wonder if people know that I'm
multitasking my mental health,
Learning how to breakdance fears
and moonwalk over worries,
Feeling like a sofa, made to be the
cemetery of coats and bags,
Never appreciated for offering
comfort for weary backs and
traveling feet,
Massive amounts of intrusive
thoughts like the red ant hill in my
driveway,
Pouring out the cement as if the
cracks were wombs,
Wombs of my distortions,

354

Giving birth to the decay of
happiness,
Depression they call it,

Making me battle 12 rounds at a time,
So tired of fighting but it taunts me,
During the intermission the patience
of past trauma hangs on to me like a
scared child at the beach for the first
time,
I shake like a wet dog but it's no use,
PTSD blows kisses to its lover OCD,
and I have become the surrogate,
Carrying the offspring of all that
troubles me,
Two sides, same coin is the life
savings from my existence,

355

Smiles and love on top of tears and
misery on repeat,

I'm a lot of things,
Like the treasure chest at the dentist
office,
I wish I could release my mind from
my head and wash it,
Hang it to dry on a clothesline like
grandma did our clothes,
but I haven't figured that part yet,
Until then I walk around like a
zombie bug,
Still doing as the living but clearly
gone,
I'm a better actor than Denzel and
Leonardo,

For my two sides of the same coin
never walks the red carpet,
Only inside my own footprints in my
house,

Made from pacing and pondering all
night,
I wish I could spend this two-sided
coin,
Buy some self-love with it,

Then hopefully my money won't be
wasted.

Chapter 9

Harlem Inspiration

359

I'm Back

Old lion leaves pride,
Young lion moves in quickly,
Old lion comes back.

Moses of North Carolina To Harlem

Who was Mr. George Moses Horton?
Born in 1798,
North Carolina,
Found his pen,
In chains and servitude,
Seen as property like the pen he
wrote with and the paper he wrote
on,
Writing his way to freedom,
First Black person published in the
South,
Tried to buy his way to freedom with
his words,
But still had to wait for Juneteenth,

361

Now my words from the same city
speak for him as he spoke for me,

My back never has taken the lash,
But built muscled thick from his
courage and heavy pen,
His dream predating the Renaissance
of Harlem,
Shining the light of the slave,
He had something to say,
Carolina born highlighting the king
within him,

186 years separates our births, but
we are still twins,
Born with the hunger for hungry
pages for us to feed,
He wrote so I could,

Through the sticky humid moonlight
to the gnat infested streetlight,
We both knew our way home,
Salute to the first to do it,
Leaving syllable prints and quill
stains for me to follow,
Thank you, Mr. Poet, Freedom looks
good on you.

From Harlem

My words are formed from what you
taught,
My joy is written from the poetry you
brought,
You came before me, and I came
from you,
Straight from Harlem where the jazz
is blue,
By reading and listening you opened
my eyes,
Now through my eyes, your wisdom
flies,
Your work equaled passion and
grace,

And now when I write, I see your
face,
Harlem, Harlem where you called
home,

Poetry now shields me like a dome,
The blow of your trombone relaxes
me,

It helps me to think and to live free,
Down in Harlem, I can hear
Langston writing,

Giving me the courage to start
striving,

Striving to be the best I can be,
Letting out with love what is inside
of me,
The roots of the creative came from
Louie,
The king of the trumpet who knew
how to boogie,
And now I enjoy art and then some,
But this enjoyment first came from
Harlem.

My Renaissance

I needed Revival of my spirit,
Redistribution of my thoughts,
Rejuvenation of dreams and hopes I
thought I had lost,
Like a Rebirth of artistry and poetic
purpose,
Reunifying passion of free verse and
rhymes,
Revitalizing my want to live,
Rehearsing my reasons to continue,
Forged and Reconstructed by the
pages of the Harlem Renaissance,
Reaching from New York all the way
to North Carolina,
I was Resuscitated mouth to mouth
by the breath of shelves and libraries,

367

**Shaping and molding and
Reinforcing the Renaissance of me.**

Baby Harlem

If I'm ever blessed with a baby girl
one day,
I hope Harlem is her name,
I hope her voice is sweet and piercing
like trumpets,
And thunder pounding like bass cord
strumming,
Her step in her walk like the
marching of rhymes and notes loud
like Calloway's band,
Her smile radiant and purposeful
like the essence of a renaissance,
Harlem will read,
Harlem will write,
Harlem will play,
Harlem will be loved,

The renewing of my life of poetry,
Born like an egg hatched with a pen
in my hand sitting on a notebook,

That's my artistic genesis,
But hers, my Harlem,
Hers will be that of the gaze of her
father,
With molecules and charismatic
sonnets formed in her heart,
Her birth will sound from the
country to the city,

With a cry like Ella, we will announce
to the world,
My baby girl, born like her daddy,
With a pen in her hand,
Nestled between loose leaf paper,

**Singing the blues and writing poems
to freedom,
My precious Harlem,
Daddy loved you way before I heard
your first notes or read your first
poem.**

Baby Langston

If I'm ever blessed to have a son, I
pray that he knows why,
Why I dreamt of him through the
chambers of the great poets,
Renaissancing the Renaissance
strong and beautiful,
I hoped for him through passages
and pages of passion filled poetry,
Never a tired eye nor rarely one that
wasn't wet with emotion and
deliverance,

I prayed for him with the same
zealousness and fervor of Claude
Mckay, Sterling Brown and James

372

Weldon Johnson's cry to be free,
truly free,

I wondered what his life would be
like as I wrestled my own,
My blues were very weary, but I
wanted more for him,
I saw my heart and mind crack open
like an egg to be scrambled,
Only to find a little yolk left,
A yolk of hope and my pen,
All I have to leave you son,

I hope it fits you because it
encapsulates the definition of rhyme
and reason,

Amplified by the anatomy of my
warrior poet spirit,
I know you will have it,
The blueprint for the encouragement
with words mighty as your father's
fist of poetic pugilistic power,
This I leave to you,
I pray for you son,

Like your name's sake, you are a
beautiful people,
From the rivers that bathed you,
Daddy loved you way before I heard
your first note,
Or read your first poem.

My Harlem Crew

Langston Hughes was in my dream
last night,
He asked if I needed his typewriter,
Zora blew me a kiss and Mr. Sterling
gave me his pencil and notebook,
I asked where I was, they whispered,
"Harlem"
Notes pulsating the floorboards like
an earthquake,
Zora yelled up to the ceiling,
"DUKE HE ALREADY AWAKE"
Helene walked in and gave me a hug,
And Claude brought the hot coffee,

Langston said, "It's time son",

As I sat down at his typewriter, I
realized what he meant,
I heard Ma Rainey's booming
thunder melodies from down the
hall,

And Louie's trumpet pierced my ears
from the other side of the hallway,
The renaissance signaled my
resurrection,

They jumped me in last night,
Said once I'm in there is no getting
out,
Salute to the Harlem Hell Fighters,
Langston said they would protect me,
and my pen,
James Weldon told me to sing,

376

So, I did, singing words knitted meticulously inspired by my new crew.

I am and It is

I am the pen serenader,
The trumpet blower,
The ink conductor,
I am the master of words,
The engineer of syllables,
The chef of metaphors,
The pilot of analogies,
I am the whisper of journals,

It is time to be heard,
It is time to be loved,
It is time to exist,

Facing the end of my notebook, I feel
rejuvenated,

378

Ready to see what blessings from
Jesus shines my way,

I am a serenader, a trumpet, a
conductor, a master, an engineer, a
chef, a pilot, and a whisper,
But most importantly,
I am a vessel poured into by the King
of Kings,

Ready to write the words of
resurrection and grace,

I am His pen and It is time.

Self-Encouragement Builds Resiliency

Thank you for reading my words, written from the quicksand.

Reviews

It has been written that "the pen is mightier than the sword," yet Reginald Wilson Jr. wields his powerful pen as a balm of encouragement and hope. Readers from diverse walks of life will joyfully resonate with his frequent references to faith, family ties, and the dignity of the Black experience. Speaking convincingly as a mental health advocate, Reggie offers validation for the struggles of anxiety, depression, trauma, and suicidal thoughts. Writing transparently as a person internally familiar with mental struggles, Reggie testifies to the deep pain we all experience, yet gently offers the antidote of self-love, truth and perseverance. His inspirational words paint vibrant images that encourage us all to make our exodus from the quicksand of hopelessness so that we can ascend to the heights of the eagle. Reggie Wilson Jr is indeed "encouragement and empathy personified."

Tonya D. Armstrong, Ph.D., M.T.S
Owner & Licensed Psychologist
The Armstrong Center for Hope
Author/Producer of *Blossoming Hope: The Black Christian Woman's Guide to Mental Health and Wellness and Blossoming Hope Companion: Soothing Songs and Spoken Word Recordings*

"Exodus From the Quicksand" is Psalms 23 to the black men of America, a fortress for male vulnerability. The fragility, the despair of loneliness, the frolic in the hope of the Lord, you will see the full man (even the sexy one) in these pages. Reggie Wilson A.K.A. The Encouraging Poet is both beauty and beast, light and dark, riddled with love for the matriarch as well as adoration for his poetic ancestors, his favorite being Langston Hughes. Remarkable courage to overcome a detrimental health battle, loss of his younger sister, and the personal hardships that come with being black in America, he is walking resilience. I am so blessed to have encountered his spirit on this journey and in these pages.

Poet Khan Rass Fiyaa

Author of *C.P.R. To My Dreams (An Ode to 2020)* as well as *My Abyss (I Wrote Him Free)*
/Poet/Publisher/Host/Friend

"The poet's job is to put into words those feelings we all have that are so deep, so important, and yet so difficult to name--to tell the truth in such a beautiful way, that people cannot live without it."-Jane Kenyon. "Depth and substance—the two most exquisite qualities, be it a poem or a person."-Sanober Khan. Reginald Wilson does his job as a poet well and is full of depth and substance. Reginald is not afraid to be vulnerable, to share his story, and to turn his pain and adversity into something strong, inspiring, and encouraging. Reginald Wilson is an amazing human, and tells the truth in such a beautiful way, that people should not live without it.

Mary Morris, MSW- Child Welfare
Coordinator and Lecturer
MSW Field Liaison

BSW Field Liaison
School of Social Work- NCSU

"Each poem in "Exodus" felt like a drama scene of a movie or play. The imagery is so heavily skilled that I had many out of body experiences. The chapters, like themes, welcome the readers into a new world of emotion and event. The biblical references and genre of mental health specifically related to black men makes one want to grab hold, appreciate, and love on the nearest black man. It is such an eloquent, deeply felt collection of "photography." Reggie did an amazing job communicating and translating "Exodus" successfully using hard hitting metaphors to reveal the overall message. "The way out is by carrying one's cross to embark on a journey of healing."

Tequila Sway, Creative Writer
Spoken Word Poet, Content Creator

Author or "Focus" self-help books

As our in-residence poet, Reggie Wilson Jr. delivers raw and courageous poetry in a style of rap that defies the modesty that lives within us all. He inspired laughter, curiosity, and sheer surprise in his offerings. In the midst of it all, the poems of innocence, reckoning, realization, and growth tugged at my heart. The ingredients in this collection are even more poignant as I continue to learn and understand the genuine and battle-tested soul from which these words sprang. These writings are pure and honest and suggest a masterful sense of self-knowledge that tolls like a bell throughout each page. Reading these sobering words made me acutely aware of the writer and myself as the reader, bound together by their healing. properties. These works resonate as the beginning of future installments, where the sun will further smile upon this poet as he continues to wade forth into a proverbial sea of all that inspires him to create and heal.

Clifton D. Garner, Sr., PsyD, LCMHCA
The Armstrong Center for Hope

Bio

Reggie Wilson Jr. is a licensed clinical social worker currently providing mental health services and is also known as THE ENCOURAGING POET. He fell in love with poetry at the age of 12 and was heavily influenced by the Harlem Renaissance. A mental health advocate who battles mental health issues himself, he can connect as only a poet therapist can. Reggie's motto is "STAY ENCOURAGED". He credits this as his motivational factor to survive and thrive.

392

Thank you Mama

Made in the USA
Columbia, SC
09 October 2024

5ac5c62f-040d-491b-a9fd-3df1d9b6eb0fR02